GREAT PEOPLE IN HISTORY

GREAT LEADERS

GREAT PEOPLE IN HISTORY
GREAT LEADERS

Brian Mooney

New York

This edition published in 2013 by:

The Rosen Publishing Group, Inc.
29 East 21st Street, New York, NY 10010

Copyright © 2013 Arcturus Publishing Limited

Library of Congress Cataloging-in-Publication Data

Mooney, Brian, 1949-
 Great leaders / Brian Mooney.
    p. cm. -- (Great people in history)
 Includes bibliographical references and index.
 ISBN 978-1-4777-0403-5 (library binding)
 1. Biography--Juvenile literature. 2. Statesmen--
Biography--Juvenile literature. 3. World history--
Juvenile literature. 4. Leadership--Juvenile literature. I.
Title.
 CT104.M65 2013
 920.073--dc23
 [B]
                                    2012032376

Manufactured in China

SL002553US

CPSIA Compliance Information: Batch W13YA:
For further information, contact Rosen Publishing,
New York, New York, at 1-800-237-9932

Contents

STATESMEN

Hatshepsut

Queen Hatshepsut was the first Queen of Egypt (c.1509–c.1469 BCE) and one of the greatest Egyptian pharaohs. She was the first powerful woman ruler in recorded history, and governed Egypt at a time of peace and commercial expansion. She sent a voyage of discovery down the Red Sea and erected two unsurpassed obelisks at the Temple of Amun in Karnak—events recorded in beautiful reliefs on her terraced temple at Deir el-Bahri.

From very early times, women in Egypt were held in high esteem. In the early 18th Dynasty there was a strong matriarchal tendency. Hatshepsut was the daughter of the great warrior king Tuthmosis I. Her half brother, Tuthmosis II, succeeded Tuthmosis I after her two brothers died

prematurely. Portrait busts show Tuthmosis II as a soft yielding boy, while Hatshepsut, several years his senior, has an erect head, bold aquiline nose, firm mouth, and chin projecting considerably to give an air of vigor and resolution. She married her half brother, reducing him to a cipher, and became the major influence in government.

After only a few years, their joint reign ended with the murder of Tuthmosis II, perhaps through a conspiracy. Hatshepsut then became regent for his son, Tuthmosis III, born of a minor woman in the harem, and, while he served as a priest of the god Amun, she took control of the throne and was accepted as pharaoh.

In inscriptions on her monuments, masculine and feminine designations of her person alternate. She is both son and daughter of Amun, the state god. Statues and reliefs show her with false beard and male dress. Though in the inscriptions masculine and feminine forms are inextricably mixed up, the personal and possessive pronouns which refer to her are feminine for the most part, with sometimes perplexing expressions such as "His Majesty herself."

As pharaoh, Hatshepsut's reign was largely peaceful, and this enabled her to carry out grand schemes of foreign commerce. Her expedition to the Land of Punt (probably modern-day Somalia) down the Red Sea can be seen as a parallel with the voyages of discovery of the European Renaissance. Her beautiful terraced mortuary temple at Deir el-Bahri has reliefs showing this expedition. It is rare that any single event of ancient history is so profusely illustrated as Hatshepsut's expedition. The various phases are recorded, from the gathering of the fleet on the Red Sea coast to the triumphant return to the capital, Thebes.

Five large ships for the voyage were built in sections and transported overland and assembled on the Red Sea coast. One of the main objectives of the expedition was to obtain incense trees; these only grow in southwest Arabia and Somalia. From reliefs on the temple at Deir el-Bahri, which show round huts on stilts accessed by ladders with coconut palms and incense trees, frankincense and myrrh, beside a copious stream with a great variety of fishes, it is believed that Punt is Somalia. Also shown are giraffes, hippopotami, apes, and dogs. The expedition was received by the prince of Punt, Parehu, and his huge sway-backed wife, Eti.

Freedom of trade was established. Egyptian goods were traded for thirty-one living incense trees, sacks of incense resin, gold, silver, ivory, ebony, cassia, kohl, apes, baboons, dogs, slaves, and leopard skins. The Queen of Punt and several chiefs accompanied the expedition back to Egypt. The arrival back in Thebes was a grand gala day. Hatshepsut offered the produce to Amun, and the incense trees were planted in the forecourt of her temple at Deir el-Bahri.

Hatshepsut's ambitious building program was far in excess of that of her predecessors. She built all over Egypt and as far as Nubia. Thebes received the most attention. The temple

Chronology

c.1509 BCE	Born, daughter of King Tuthmosis I
c.1490–1468 BCE	Rules as pharaoh in the 18th Dynasty
Year 7 of reign	Grandiose scheme for temple at Deir el-Bahri started
Year 9	Expedition to Punt
Years 15–16	Quarrying and erection of a pair of obelisks at Karnak
Years 20–21, (c.1469 BCE)	Kingship reverts to Tuthmosis III; Hatshepsut disappears from history

at Deir el-Bahri was called "Holy of Holies" and was Hatshepsut's most complete statement in material form about her reign. She cut a tomb for herself in the Valley of the Kings, and the Temple of Amun at Karnak was expanded.

The pride of her work at Karnak was two obelisks of red granite, carved from the quarries at Aswan in seven months, which are unexcelled in form, color, and beauty of engraving. Reliefs on the temple at Deir el-Bahri show the giant barge built of sycamore wood with the two obelisks on board being towed down the Nile by numerous boats. It is astounding that these obelisks, almost 100 feet (30 meters) tall, were taken on and off the barge and moved into position in the temple at Karnak. The obelisks are covered with the most delicately finished hieroglyphics, in which Hatshepsut declares that they are erected to the glory of Amun and to the memory of Tuthmosis I, each "one block of hard granite, without seam, without joining together." The entire shafts and summits of the obelisks were gilded.

Hatshepsut's ambitious building program far exceeded that of her predecessors

Meanwhile, Tuthmosis III had grown to be the energetic head of the army. Somewhere about Year 18 of Hatshepsut's reign, several of her most prominent supporters disappeared from view, and sometime in Year 20 or 21, c.1469 BCE, she too vanished from history. She was about forty years old and had ruled for twenty-two years.

A Master Builder

■ Hatshepsut attained unprecedented power for a queen. Her reign was mainly peaceful, with little war, allowing her to concentrate on improving the lot of her people. She inaugurated building projects that far outstripped those of her predecessors, including the magnificent temple at Deir el-Bahri. The temple is Hatshepsut's supreme achievement and her most enduring monument, containing scenes and inscriptions of important projects and events in her life.

■ Although one of the obelisks at the Temple of Amun has fallen, the one to the north is still in its original position, the tallest standing obelisk in Egypt.

Pericles

Pericles (c.495–429 BCE) was an Athenian statesman and general under whose rule Greek civilization reached its zenith. So great an influence did he wield over Greek life that the time of his rule is known as the Age of Pericles.

He was brought up in the shadow of war in a military household; he was only three years old when the Persians made their first bid to conquer the Greeks and were soundly defeated at Marathon, and his father was the army commander Xanthippus, who overwhelmed the Persians at Mycale in 479 BCE after they had invaded Greece for the second time and sacked Athens. The Persians were beaten off again seven years later at Salamis in 472 BCE. It was this battle that indirectly gave Pericles, by now a young, cultured intellectual, his first break.

In 472 BCE, Pericles sponsored a hugely successful dramatic production for the festival of Dionysus—a major annual event in Athens. It was the play *The Persians* by Aeschylus, the first of the great tragic playwrights, and it won first prize and brought Pericles to widespread public prominence.

A Greek Orator

Extracts from Pericles' funeral oration for the dead of the first year of the Peloponnesian War:

■ "The man who can most truly be counted brave is he who best knows the meaning of what is sweet in life and what is terrible; and then goes out undeterred to meet what is to come."

■ "Our love of what is beautiful does not lead to extravagance; our love of the things of the mind does not make us soft."

■ "We regard wealth as something to be properly used, rather than as something to boast about."

Chronology

c.495 BCE	Born in Athens
472 BCE	Produces *The Persians*
461 BCE	Leads vote against the Areopagus
451 BCE	New citizenship law
431 BCE	Peloponnesian War
429 BCE	Death of Pericles

His first real involvement in politics began a decade later, in 461 BCE, when he joined forces with a radical politician called Ephialtes to organize a vote in the popular assembly that would deprive the Areopagus, the old noble council, of its remaining power. It was a defining moment in Athenian democracy, one that is as relevant today as it was then; henceforth laws would be determined by the votes of the people, rather than by hereditary powers.

The move sparked a backlash in which Ephialtes was assassinated, and thrust Pericles into the center of Athenian politics. In 458 BCE he was elected *strategos*, effectively master of the city-state—a position he held on and off for much of the next thirty years. During his time in office, he forged Athens into a "superstate," extended her empire and expanded her sea power (sometimes at the head of his own forces), negotiated a final peace with Persia, and introduced payment for jury service. This allowed poorer people, who could otherwise not afford to leave their work, to take part in public life.

In 451 BCE Pericles introduced a new citizenship law which barred the children of non-Athenian parents from becoming full citizens. Pericles also instigated a great rebuilding program of temples and public buildings, which transformed Athens into the most magnificent city of the ancient world.

Pericles was always his own man. He commanded the popular assembly with his superb oratory but remained aloof from society and shunned social gatherings; he is reported to have attended only one in his adult life—and then he left early. He refused to accept "gifts," as was the normal custom for politicians. But he did what he wanted in his own private life. He divorced his wife and scandalized polite Athenian society by taking up with a beautiful foreign hostess, Aspasia. What shocked most was that Pericles treated Aspasia as an equal— even though they were not married. Socrates described her as one of the most intelligent and witty women of her time.

Pericles' last years were dogged by war, which was partially of his own making; the splendor and power he had achieved for Athens had sparked the jealousy of the other Greek city-states, especially Sparta, and the Peloponnesian War broke out in 431 BCE. The countryside around Athens was ravaged, and plague swept the city, shattering Athenian confidence. Pericles was deposed from office and subjected to a sham trial, but he was reelected in 429 BCE.

Pericles died of plague soon after—a year before the Parthenon was inaugurated. But his real monument was to have created an intellectual and cultural environment which nurtured the disparate geniuses of Anaxagoras and Socrates, Euripides, Aeschylus, and Sophocles, Pindar and Pheidias, Antiphon and Aristophanes, Democritus and Hippocrates, Herodotus and Thucydides. They all lived in or came to Athens in the Age of Pericles, and many were his friends.

During his time in office, Pericles expanded the city-state of Athens into a superstate

Ashoka

Ashoka (300–232 BCE) was first of the great rulers of India. After renouncing violence and embracing Buddhism, Ashoka reigned over his empire with an unwavering respect for the sanctity of human life. In effect, he introduced a completely new social philosophy.

Ashoka was the third king of the Maurya dynasty, which ruled much of the Indian subcontinent from its northern capital in Pataliputra, modern Patna. He lived lavishly and self-indulgently until he went to war to conquer the east-coast kingdom of the Kalingas, the modern Indian province of Orissa. The horrors of the war in which, by his own accounts, 100,000 were slain made such an impact on him that he renounced violence and became a Buddhist monk. For the next three decades, as monk and king, he ruled benignly over a peaceful and prosperous empire.

Our knowledge of Ashoka comes down to us in a series of edicts in which he sets out the theory and practice of a new social ethic. The edicts, in Prakrit for the Indian population and in Greek and Aramaic for the people in the northwest of his empire, were inscribed on rock surfaces or pillars.

The Dhauli stone near Bhubineswar records the king's "profound sorrow and regret" at the slaughter of the war against the Kalingas. The edicts are underpinned by his complete acceptance of the Buddhist dharma, the law of piety, right living and morality; he promoted what he called "conquest by dharma" (Universal Law). "The law of piety; to wit, obedience to father and mother; liberality to friends, acquaintances,

The Edicts

- The Major Rock Edicts and the Pillar Edicts are the most comprehensive of all the Buddhist doctrines of Ashoka, and stress the importance of religious and ideological tolerance, nonviolence, justice, and harmony in relationships.
- The Minor Edicts relate Ashoka's commitment to Buddhism.
- Ashoka's full name was Ashokavardhana. In most inscriptions he is called King Priyadarsin.
- The lion capital of the Ashoka Pillar (pictured right) found at Sarnath is India's national emblem.

relatives, Brahmins, and ascetics; respect for sacredness of life; avoidance of violence and extravagance and violence of language."

Ashoka all but eliminated the unnecessary slaughter of animals, even curtailing fishing. He appointed ministers to ensure that the dharma was observed, and sent missionaries abroad as far as Syria and Egypt to preach its message.

In a blueprint for his provincial officers Ashoka states: "There are, however, certain dispositions which render success impossible, namely, envy, lack of perseverance, harshness, impatience, want of application, idleness, indolence. You therefore should desire to be free from such dispositions."

He had similar strictures for himself: "I have accordingly arranged that at all hours and in all places—whether I am dining or in

Chronology

300 BCE Born
273 BCE Ashoka accedes to the throne
269 BCE Ashoka crowned king
264 BCE War against the kingdom of the Kalingas
260 BCE Ashoka becomes a Buddhist monk
232 BCE Dies

the ladies' apartments, in my bedroom or in my closet, in my carriage, or in the palace gardens—the official reporters shall keep me constantly informed of the people's business, which business of the people I am ready to dispose of at any place" and "Work I must for the public benefit."

This was not just pious propaganda. The edicts have a refreshing ring of frankness and sincerity, and Ashoka practiced what he preached. He went on frequent tours around his empire to spread his teaching. He looked after the welfare of his subjects by building an extensive network of road communications, planting the sides of the roads with shady banyan trees, providing roadside wells, setting up free rest houses, cultivating medicinal plants, and founding hospitals—both for sick people, his subjects, and for animals.

Ashoka seemed to be particularly aware of the needs of women and the plight of the rural poor. He upheld the principle of religious freedom, saying he had achieved more by persuasion than by commands. Few leaders since him—perhaps none—have ruled with such a record of tolerance.

While Ashoka's rule of piety did not last long after his death, he himself gave India an unprecedented time of peace and prosperity and helped ensure that Buddhism and its teaching spread throughout the world.

Ashoka's edicts, far from being simply pious propaganda, have a refreshing ring of sincerity

Qin Shi Huangdi

Qin Shi Huangdi (259–210 BCE) unified China's warring states under the Qin or Ch'in dynasty, founded the Chinese Empire, and became its first Emperor.

The future emperor was born in 259 BCE in the state of Qin, in northwestern China. His name was Ying Zheng, and he was officially the son of Zhuang Xiang, the future king of Qin, one of China's seven feudal states. His father became king in 246 BCE when Zheng was thirteen but died soon after, and for the next seven years his mother and a wealthy merchant Lü Buwei served as regents. In the wake of a scandal involving his mother and a man who had pretended to be a eunuch, and an attempted revolt, Zheng took control of his kingdom and set about expanding it. His first act on becoming king was to execute his mother's lover and exile Lü.

He was a ruthlessly brutal dictator, and, with the help of good generals, bribery, and bullying, before he was forty he had unified the warring states of China and forged them into a single empire; in 221 BCE he took the title Qin Shi Huangdi—"First Emperor of Qin."

By most accounts, Qin Shi Huangdi was a nasty piece of work. He would mete out cruel punishments, and he organized one of history's first public book burnings in 213 BCE when all works outside the imperial library of a "non-technical" nature were ordered to be burnt—a brutal attempt to eliminate the teachings of Confucian scholars, who opposed the emperor's reforms. Thousands of dissenting scholars were buried alive. In later life, having survived three attempted assassinations, he lived in terror of death. He would travel with two identical carriages and never sleep the night in the same place. He made extensive tours of his empire but otherwise shut himself up in his palaces, increasingly remote from his people. He sent out agents and went himself in search of elixirs of eternal life; he turned to alchemists with the same hope.

But he also achieved many remarkable things for China; above all, he established the structures

A Terracotta Army

■ Apart from the legacy of the name of China, named after the Qin or Ch'in dynasty, another of Qin's legacies lay undiscovered for more than 2,000 years. In 1974 farmers digging a well outside the present-day capital, X'ian, near the First Emperor's tomb, stumbled across the gravesite of an entire army made of terracotta. Archeologists subsequently discovered four underground chambers containing some 7,000 life-size soldiers and horses—buried there to protect the emperor in the afterlife.

■ Qin Shi Huangdi was responsible for the construction of the major section—nearly 1,200 miles (1,900 kilometers)—of the Great Wall of China, one of the largest man-made objects in existence.

of a modern state. He abolished territorial feudal power, and divided the country into thirty-six separately governed states; he gave his empire a single currency, standardized weights and measurements, a uniform legal system, and a common written language. He also fostered religion. He built a network of roads and canals and, to protect the country against marauding Huns, he set up defensive military forces, and he ordered the construction of the major portion of the Great Wall of China.

A ruthless dictator, before he was forty Qin had unified the warring Chinese states in a single empire

He proclaimed that his dynasty would last 10,000 generations, while in fact it only survived four years after his death; but the centralized state he set up was the basis of Imperial China until its end in 1911, and in many respects lives on in another guise today.

Chronology

259 BCE Born Ying Zheng
246 BCE Inherits throne on death of his father
238 BCE Becomes king
221 BCE Takes title Qin Shi Huangdi, "First Emperor"
210 BCE Dies of natural causes

Augustus

Augustus, the first Emperor of Rome (63 BCE–14 CE), restored unity and order to Rome, and founded an empire that was to last longer than any other in European history. His reign bridged two epochs, and brought a period of unrivaled peace, prosperity, and culture—the Augustan age.

Gaius Octavius, as he was born, was an unknown twenty-year-old soldier, scholar, and religious official when he received the alarming news that his great-uncle Julius Caesar had been assassinated, and the even more disturbing news that Caesar had nominated him as his successor. It would take seventeen years of fighting and intrigue to consolidate his power.

He changed his name to Julius Caesar Octavianus, to draw on popular support for his great-uncle and adoptive father, became Consul, and initially fought and then formed an alliance with Mark Antony, Caesar's ambitious colleague, and his ally General Marcus Lepidus. This three-man military junta, the Second Triumvirate, began with brutal violence, a proscription in which thousands of opponents, among them 200 senators and the orator Cicero, were killed. It was a fractured peace. After putting down a challenge from Pompey's surviving son, Sextus, Octavian then drove out Lepidus. Mark Antony, in the East, always posed the ultimate challenge, which came to a head after he married Cleopatra, Queen of Egypt. Octavian defeated their joint forces at the naval battle of Actium in 31 BCE and consolidated his hold by taking control of the East.

The Senate conferred the title Caesar Augustus on Octavian in 27 BCE, and, with more powers and honors to come, he spent the next forty-one years as the virtually undisputed ruler of Rome and her huge territories. But he was careful never to take on the trappings of a monarch, cleverly masking his dictatorial powers through various constitutional settlements, deals with the Senate, and proconsular arrangements; with an abuse of language that would not have been out of place in Stalin's Russia, Augustus referred to himself as "first citizen."

He was a complex character: ruthless at the outset and harsh, even to his own children—"a chill and mature terrorist," said one opponent—but also magnanimous, tolerant, tactful, approachable, upright, and hard-working. In the final analysis, he was a skillfully manipulative politician and a master of propaganda.

A great builder, Augustus literally transformed Rome. "I found Rome a city of bricks and left it

> *"I found Rome a city of bricks, and left it a city of marble"*

"Unusually Handsome"

■ Augustus' appearance was a natural gift to sculptors, coin makers, and medalists—"unusually handsome...his hair slightly curly and inclining to golden," wrote his biographer Suetonius. "He had clear bright eyes, in which he liked to have it thought there was a divine power."

■ Augustus was the author of many works (all lost)—including a pamphlet against Brutus, a treatise on philosophy, and an account of his early life and poems.

■ Some of his architectural monuments can still be seen in Rome: the Theater of Marcellus; the colonnaded Forum with its Temple of Mars the Avenger; and his own mausoleum.

Chronology

63 BCE Born in Rome, September 23
47 BCE Raised to College of Pontifices
44 BCE Nominated heir to Caesar
43 BCE Second Triumvirate
31 BCE Battle of Actium
27 BCE Senate confers on him title Caesar
Augustus
14 CE Dies at Nola, Italy, August 19

a city of marble," he said. He also left behind an impressive network of roads. He was a patron of the arts, and a friend of the poets Ovid, Horace, and Virgil, as well as the historian Livy.

He strategically shifted the focus of the empire to the west, and pushed roads, garrisons, and troops to the borders of the provinces, which benefited enormously from his reign. The resulting *Pax Romana*, based on easy communications and flourishing trade, and underpinned by what was now a professional army, was to provide western Europe, the Middle East, and the North African seaboard with the longest period of unity, peace, and prosperity in their entire recorded history.

At home he reorganized practically every aspect of Roman life. He overhauled the whole apparatus of government, created a more permanent civil service over which he had control, and instigated new laws, even attempting to improve public morality through stricter laws on marriage and a ban on displays of extravagance. Augustus married three times; his third wife was Livia Drusilla. His last years were overshadowed by the successive deaths of those he had selected as his successors. He was eventually succeeded by his stepson Tiberius, the natural son of Livia.

Constantine the Great

Constantine the Great (280–337), Roman emperor, was the first Roman ruler to convert to and legalize Christianity, and he was also the founder of Constantinople (present-day Istanbul). He laid the foundations of Christian European civilization.

Born in Naissus, the modern Nish in Serbia, Flavius Valerius Constantinus was the son of a military commander, Constantius Chlorus, who rose to be co-emperor, and of a woman of humble background, Helena, who was canonized a saint. Constantius died in 306 in York, England, where he had been campaigning against the Picts accompanied by his son, who was immediately proclaimed co-emperor in his place. It would take Constantine eighteen years, however, before he finally established himself as sole ruler in 324.

Constantine's conversion to Christianity was almost certainly a gradual process, but the trigger was what he believed was a vision he had in 312, on the eve of the Battle of the Milvian Bridge, in which Christ told him to inscribe the first two letters of his name (XP in Greek) on the shield of his troops. Constantine obeyed the vision, and took his subsequent decisive victory over his rival Maxentius as a sign from "the God of the Christians." Persecution of Christians was ended, and Constantine and his co-emperor Licinius issued what has come to be called the Edict of Milan, an edict of "tolerance," in 313, which de facto legalized Christianity throughout the Roman Empire. Constantine became a Christian, though not Licinius.

An armed struggle for power soon began between Licinius and Constantine, from which Constantine emerged victorious in 324, as Emperor of both East and West, and as champion of Christianity. He involved himself more and more in ecclesiastical affairs, and convened the Council of Nicaea in order to get the Church Fathers to agree on a unified teaching. Out of Nicaea came the Nicene Creed, still a primary prayer for all Christian believers. A lavish builder, Constantine founded the basilicas in Rome of St Peter's and St John Lateran, and, in a momentous decision, he built a monumental new capital for the empire at the small town of Byzantium. It was called Constantinople in his honor, and is today's glorious Istanbul.

Constantine was only baptized into the Church on his deathbed, a sign, his critics say, of a cynical, half-hearted approach to Christianity. In fact there is abundant evidence that he was sincere in his faith: he had enforced the observance of Sunday as a day of rest, he had his children educated as Christians, and surviving letters concerning the Church in North Africa attest to a deep personal commitment. Moreover, late baptism was quite normal in the early Christian Church.

The Holy Sepulcher

■ Constantine's mother Helena made a pilgrimage to Jerusalem in 326; in a tradition more cherished than trustworthy, she is revered for unearthing the cross on which Christ was crucified at the spot where her son founded the Basilica of the Holy Sepulcher. The basilica is still there—down the centuries the object of endless feuds between different Christian churches.

■ Did the Christian Church ever regain its purity after being legalized by Constantine? The Church lost the independence it had previously enjoyed, and it became an instrument of imperial policy and part of the establishment—an awkward status that has haunted it for centuries and that remains even today in some countries, including England.

Chronology

280	Born at Naissus on February 27
306	Proclaimed co-emperor
312	Battle of the Milvian Bridge
313	Edict of Milan de facto legalizing Christianity
325	Council of the Church at Nicaea
326	Constantinople founded
337	Dies on May 22, two weeks after being baptized

But Constantine was also a product of his age and he could be both brutal and cruel. Even after his conversion, he had his brother-in-law, Licinius, executed, and Licinius's son, Licinianus, flogged to death. Constantine also had his wife, Fausta, suffocated in a superheated bath, and their son, Crispus, put to the sword. He maintained a certain ambivalence toward pagan practice, both as an expedient and a sign of genuine tolerance; he was also generous and did much for children, women, and slaves.

In other fields, Constantine was not a great innovator, but he restored the empire's economy to a modicum of prosperity; he introduced a new gold coinage and imposed an unpopular new tax. He reformed both the civil administration and the professional army; his reign was marked by unbroken military success. But Constantine's lasting achievements were Christian Europe and the Eastern Empire.

Constantine's lasting achievements were Christian Europe and the Eastern Empire

Justinian I

Justinian I (483–565) was a Byzantine emperor who earned the title Great by reestablishing the old Roman Empire in the West, but his lasting achievement was to codify Roman law. His Codex Justinianus remains the basis for the law of most European countries.

Born Flavius Petrus Sabbatius of poor peasant stock in what is today Serbia, Justinian owed his advancement to his uncle, Emperor Justin I, after whom he took his name. Educated in Constantinople, capital of the Eastern Empire, he became Justin's administrator and was nominated his successor in 518. He was elected Emperor on his uncle's death in 527.

The energetic Justinian set himself an ambitious goal—to recover the territories lost to invaders and restore the tattered Roman Empire and revive its glory. Italy, Spain, and Rome's former North African provinces were in the hands of Vandal and Gothic tribes, the Slavs were encroaching from the north, and Persia pressing from the east. Justinian was fortunate in his choice of military commander: General Belisarius was commander in chief for most of Justinian's reign, and he was more than a match for the new emperor's ambitions.

Justinian was a prodigious builder: more than any other he refined and perfected Byzantine architecture

Heading a force of just 18,000 men, Belisarius recaptured North Africa from the Vandals in 533. He next landed in southern Italy and retook Rome from the Ostrogoths in 536 but, although most of the peninsula was back under Roman rule by 540, it would take until 552 before the last Gothic strongholds were overrun. Southeastern Spain fell more easily, and by the end of Justinian's reign the Mediterranean was, for the most part, once again a Roman sea. Campaigns against the Persians checked their advances, and the Roman frontier was pushed back so the shores of the Black Sea were once again secured. Justinian was no less successful at home; in 532, Belisarius had put down the so-called Nika revolt, sparked by rival teams of chariot racers—the Blues and Greens—who staged a major insurrection.

Justinian's vision of strong empire called for a uniform legal system. He appointed an imperial commission, headed by the jurist Tribonian, to

A Jealous Emperor

■ Belisarius, who rose to prominence fighting against the Persians, recaptured Rome from the Vandals for Justinian on two occasions. He held the city for a year and nine days (536–7) against a far larger Gothic force, famously defending the Aurelian walls by breaking statues and dropping them on the attackers.

■ Justinian was jealous of Belisarius. Afraid that his general would seize the throne, he recalled him early from Italy. In 542 he accused him of disloyalty and stripped him of his command. Belisarius was reinstated and sent back to Rome, but was jailed again for conspiracy in 562. He was, however, quickly released and allowed to live peacefully in retirement. The general died in 565, the same year as the emperor.

■ Justinian's reign was marked by a succession of earthquakes and other natural disasters. The bubonic plague that was to ravage Europe in future generations first appeared in Constantinople in 542.

collect and systematize a thousand years of Roman laws. The task took ten years and resulted in the Codex Justinianus—the Justinian Code—which was published in four separate collections and then promulgated in its entirety in 534. The resulting work, which included a manual for law students, meant that for the first time Roman laws were logically arranged, so that every citizen could find out easily the law of the empire on any subject. The codification was Justinian's great work.

Justinian was also a prodigious builder and, more than any others, he refined and perfected the style that is Byzantine architecture. He covered the empire from Ravenna to Damascus with superb monuments, the pride among them being the Church of Our Lady in Jerusalem, which is now the Al-Aqsa Mosque, and the great Basilica of St Sophia (Hagia Sophia) in Constantinople. The emperor himself shines out in a portrait, standing in his toga and surrounded by his court, in the magnificent mosaics in San Vitale at Ravenna.

Justinian married a beautiful former dancing girl, Theodora, in 523. Scandal pursued her, but Theodora provided crucial support to the emperor in times of crisis, notably the Nika revolt in 532.

Although Justinian's great conquests were not sustained by his successors, and his reunification of the Roman Empire proved fleeting, his legacy in law and Byzantine architecture would live on.

Chronology

483	Born in Tauresium, Dardania (Serbia)
518	Named as Justin's successor
527	Justinian elected Emperor
532	Nika insurrection put down
533	North Africa recaptured
534	*Codex Justinianus* promulgated
536	Rome retaken
540	Gothic capital of Ravenna falls
565	Dies at Constantinople, November 14

Charlemagne

Charlemagne (742–814) was the first ruler of Europe. King of the Franks and later Holy Roman Emperor, during forty years of military campaigns he expanded an empire that stretched from the Atlantic to the Danube, and from the Netherlands to Provence.

Charlemagne was a giant of a man: over six feet (1.8 m) tall, strongly built with lively eyes, a long nose, long moustaches, and fair hair. His father, Pepin the Short, had difficulty maintaining the Frankish empire which Charlemagne's grandfather, Charles Martel, had reunited. Pepin had deposed the Merovingian King of Gaul and made himself King of the Franks, and on his death in 768 the kingdom was shared between Charlemagne and his older brother Carloman.

Carloman died in 771 and Charlemagne reunited the kingdom, ignoring his nephews' rights. Charlemagne was primarily a great warrior leader, who in fifty-three campaigns extended the Frankish empire over most of present-day Europe and established Christianity over the pagans of central Europe. Wars gave him power because he distributed land and booty to his followers. Thus rewarded, his vassals were appointed as regional governors. Envoys checked that they were not oppressive, and because most of society was illiterate many clerics were employed as officials.

Charlemagne established a Christian Frankish empire over the pagan peoples of Europe

In 774 Charlemagne invaded Lombardy (northern Italy), whose king supported Carloman's widow, and in 775 he began his campaigns against the Saxons, which lasted over thirty years. In 778 he besieged Zaragoza to help Arab rebels of the Emir of Cordoba. He deposed his cousin the Duke of Bavaria in 788, and began subduing other German tribes before taking on Hungary and Austria.

Charlemagne strengthened the alliance between the Roman papacy and the kingdom of

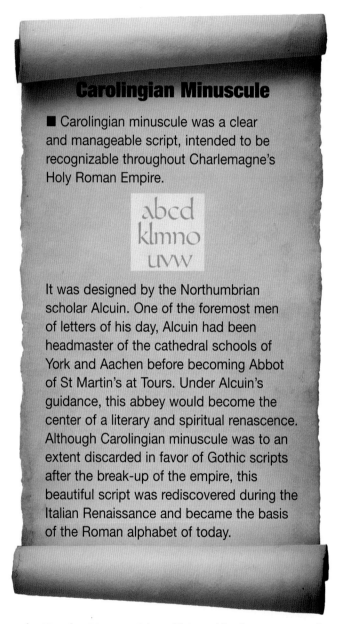

Carolingian Minuscule

■ Carolingian minuscule was a clear and manageable script, intended to be recognizable throughout Charlemagne's Holy Roman Empire.

abcd
klmno
uvw

It was designed by the Northumbrian scholar Alcuin. One of the foremost men of letters of his day, Alcuin had been headmaster of the cathedral schools of York and Aachen before becoming Abbot of St Martin's at Tours. Under Alcuin's guidance, this abbey would become the center of a literary and spiritual renascence. Although Carolingian minuscule was to an extent discarded in favor of Gothic scripts after the break-up of the empire, this beautiful script was rediscovered during the Italian Renaissance and became the basis of the Roman alphabet of today.

the Franks. He considered himself to be appointed by God to look after the temporal and spiritual well-being of his people. He held the papacy in high regard, and protected it from territorial incursions. All churches in his kingdoms used the same Roman liturgy, a strong unifying factor. He therefore reacted angrily to the 787 Council of Nicaea decrees settling the iconoclast heresy. He had not been invited to attend the council,

so he held his own synod in Frankfurt to decide the matter. In 800 Pope Leo III was deposed and escaped to Charlemagne's court. Later that year Charlemagne restored the pope, who in return crowned him first Holy Roman Emperor on Christmas Day. Not until 812 did the Byzantine Emperor Michael I recognize Charlemagne's title as Emperor of the West, maintaining that the Eastern Empire was the true heir of Rome.

Charlemagne spoke Latin and some Greek, and was a great patron of learning, although he was himself probably illiterate. Alcuin, a noted scholar from Northumbria in the north of England, was persuaded to preside over the palace school where both girls and boys were taught. Illuminated manuscripts and ivory carvings reflect his patronage of the arts. He was a pioneer of Romanesque architecture, although his great chapel at Aachen reflects the Byzantine church of San Vitale in Ravenna, which he had visited and admired. He built a bridge over the Rhine, and a canal linking the Rhine and Danube rivers.

Charlemagne died in 814 aged seventy, leaving Europe with a dream of unity. Shortly after his death the Treaty of Verdun split Charlemagne's empire three ways: future France and Germany, and the "Middle Kingdom" (Alsace Lorraine), which became a persistent problem well into the twentieth century.

Chronology

742	Born in Aachen, now Germany, April 2
768	Becomes joint ruler with brother of Frankish kingdoms
773	Invades and conquers Lombardy
775	Begins campaigning in Saxony
787	Holds own Synod of Frankfurt when not invited to Council of Nicaea
788	Conquers Bavaria
796	Campaigns in Hungary
800	Crowned first Holy Roman Emperor
814	Dies in Aachen, January 28

Mehmed II

Mehmed II (1432–81), the conqueror of Constantinople and Sultan of Ottoman Turkey, was the true founder of Ottoman imperial power, which lasted more than 400 years.

The Turkish Ottomans, originally nomads from Central Asia, had already conquered large swathes of the eastern Mediterranean and Balkans by the time of Mehmed's birth in 1432. The fourth son of Murad II and a slave girl, he was set on the throne in 1444, aged only twelve. But the Ottomans were still vulnerable to attack from Christian Europe; Mehmed's father had to come out of retirement to beat off a Crusader army at the battle of Varna. He then took back the throne until his death in 1451.

Mehmed, meanwhile, had nurtured an ambition to take Constantinople, a strategic stronghold on the shores of two seas and the crossroads between two continents, which had been the outpost of the Eastern Roman Empire since it was founded by Constantine the Great in 324, and the headquarters of the Eastern Christian Church. The Ottomans had their capital in a far more humble setting at Edirne, 200 miles (320 km) northwest of the Golden City.

The twenty-year-old sultan prepared for the siege and assault with single-minded determination and remarkable skill—he reinforced his army and bought off Venice and Hungary with favorable treaties. He erected a fortress on the edge of the city's great walls at Rumeli Hisar, cast the largest-caliber cannons that had ever been fired, and built a fleet to control the Bosporus. The siege lasted from April 2 to May 29, 1453, and in the end neither the huge cannon nor the sight of impaled Christians broke the defenders but Mehmed's orders for the fleet to be dragged overland behind Pera and into the Golden Horn proved a masterstroke; the city lost its harbor. On the day of the final attack Mehmed personally directed his crack soldiers, the janissaries, through one of the breaches in the city wall. The city was looted, and contemporary chroniclers spoke of rivers of blood. The last Roman emperor, Constantine XI, died fighting; it was the end of the Roman Empire. Mehmed, himself, went straight to the cathedral of Hagia Sophia, the mother church of Eastern Christendom, and converted it into a mosque.

The capture of Constantinople bestowed immense glory and prestige on Mehmed: he was the champion of Islam, heir to Alexander the Great and the Roman Caesars, and Padishah, "Sovereign of the Two Lands and the Two Seas." Mehmed gave back to Constantinople in equal measure: he established a truly cosmopolitan

Chroniclers of Mehmed's seizure of Constantinople spoke of "rivers of blood" during the city's capture

A Cultured Tyrant

■ Although he was cruel and meted out dreadful punishment, Mehmed was a man of great culture, and he was remarkably broadminded. He read widely and also wrote poetry.

■ He asked the patriarch Gennadius Scholarius to write a treatise on the Christian faith and had it translated into Turkish.

■ He invited the artist Gentile Bellini from Venice to decorate the walls of his palace with frescos. Bellini painted a portrait of Mehmed, which is in the National Gallery in London.

■ Mehmed's janissaries were the elite footsoldiers, the shock troops, who won the Ottoman Empire. The word comes from yeni ceri, Turkish for "new troops."

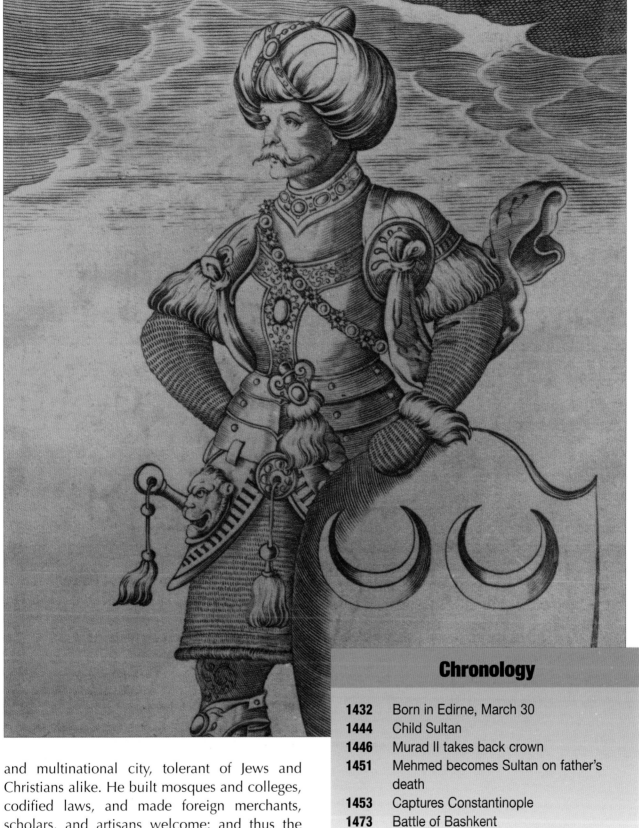

Chronology

1432	Born in Edirne, March 30
1444	Child Sultan
1446	Murad II takes back crown
1451	Mehmed becomes Sultan on father's death
1453	Captures Constantinople
1473	Battle of Bashkent
1481	Dies near Constantinople, May 3

and multinational city, tolerant of Jews and Christians alike. He built mosques and colleges, codified laws, and made foreign merchants, scholars, and artisans welcome; and thus the imperial Byzantine traditions, with their Greek and Roman legacies, were opaquely distilled into a new Turkish Ottoman reality.

For the rest of his reign, Mehmed continued the expansion of Ottoman rule in a series of successful military expeditions, as far afield as the Crimea and southern Italy. He sealed Ottoman domination of Anatolia and the Balkans in a decisive victory over the Turkmen leader Uzun Hasan at the Battle of Bashkent in 1473, and he was planning to invade Italy when he died.

Süleyman I

Süleyman I, the Magnificent (1494–1566) was the greatest of the Ottoman sultans. He extended Ottoman rule from Baghdad to central Europe and set new standards for Ottoman civilization in law, literature, art, and architecture.

The son of Sultan Selim I and a slave girl, Süleyman gained experience as a provincial governor before succeeding his father as sultan in 1520. He inherited a crack army and he used it to good effect for much of his reign. He carried Ottoman arms far into Europe: Belgrade was captured in 1521 and the Hungarians defeated at the Battle of Mohács in 1526,

Chronology

1494	Born in Trabzon (Trebizond), November 6
1521	Captures Belgrade
1520	Becomes Sultan
1526	Defeats Hungary at battle of Mochas
1529	Lays siege to Vienna
1538	Ottoman fleet defeats Spanish and Venetians
1566	Dies in Szigetvár, Hungary, September 6

At home, Süleyman appointed a succession of able grand viziers, and employed architects to embellish Constantinople and cities like Baghdad with mosques, bridges, and aqueducts. His chief architect Sinan built the Süleymaniye Mosque and its complex of colleges, libraries, shops, and hospitals, and the Shehzade Mosque, buildings that transformed classical Constantinople into Muslim Istanbul. Sinan built or restored 477 buildings, of which 319 were in Constantinople. Süleyman's court was famed for its splendor and for its elaborate oriental rituals, and his gilded and bejeweled throne room left visitors in awe. Grand public celebrations to mark the circumcision of his sons in 1530 lasted fifty-five days. Poetry also flourished during his reign, and many new laws were enacted, earning Süleyman the posthumous title of the "Law Giver." It was in every respect a golden age.

after Süleyman crossed the Drava River on a bridge of boats, which he burnt behind him. Süleyman's armies went back and forth into Hungary many times during his reign to settle dynastic rivalries in the conquered land. In 1529, Süleyman unsuccessfully laid siege to Vienna, the East European capital of his Habsburg rival Emperor Charles V. But Süleyman eventually extracted tribute from Emperor Charles and he forged a close alliance with France; he made the Ottomans count in Europe.

Süleyman waged three major campaigns against Persia, and took Iraq, adding the dazzling Muslim city of Baghdad to his empire. Under Süleyman, the Ottomans became the leading power in the Mediterranean. Early in his reign he seized Rhodes from the Knights of St John of Jerusalem but soon realized that he needed a navy to match his ambitions. He built one with the help of Algerian corsairs under the leadership of Khayr ad-Din, known in the West as Barbarossa, who was made admiral of the Ottoman fleet in 1534. The Ottoman fleet overcame the combined fleets of Venice and Spain in 1538 and helped extend Ottoman rule through most of North Africa. Barbarossa died in 1546, but his mighty navy continued to pluck prizes—Tripoli in 1551 and Djerba in 1560. There were just two major setbacks: they failed to take Oran and were repulsed from Malta by the Knights of St John.

Under Süleyman, the Ottoman Turks would become the leading power in the Mediterranean

The Warrior Poet

■ Süleyman was an accomplished poet, leaving behind no fewer than 2,000 ghazals, short poems, most of them to his Polish-born wife Hürrem, to whom he remained devoted and faithful. She was a power in the palace.

■ One of his verses to her starts: "The green of my garden, my sweet sugar, my treasure, my love."

■ Baqi (1520–99), the sultan of poets, was Süleyman's favorite.

■ The main business of the Ottoman state was war. Its governing class was known as soldiers (*askeris*), and the army was dominant. The Ottomans employed mercenaries and slaves like the janissaries, who could rise to high rank on merit alone.

■ "Day and night our horse is saddled and our saber is girt," Süleyman once boasted. This was no idle boast: Süleyman died in 1566 on his thirteenth campaign, and seventh in Hungary, while besieging the Hungarian fortress of Szigetvár.

Tokugawa Ieyasu

Tokugawa Ieyasu (1543–1616), samurai war lord and statesman, founded Japan's Tokugawa dynasty of shoguns that ended more than a century of feuding and lasted more than 250 years.

In the early sixteenth century, Japan was an anarchy of feuding clans, in which the future Shogun was caught up as a child. Originally named Matsudaira Takechiyo, Ieyasu was born into the Matsudaira military clan in Mikawa near the modern city of Nagoya, and at the age of seven he was sent as a hostage to cement an alliance with the neighboring Imagawa family, who were headquartered at Sumpu (Shizuoka).

Ieyasu built the largest castle in the world in its day—Edo— on the site of present-day Tokyo

He grew up at Sumpu, receiving an education and military training; he also developed a love of falconry. Later, he started leading military expeditions for Imagawa Yoshimoto; over the years he was to become a fearless samurai warrior. He also married and fathered the first of many sons.

Imagawa Yoshimoto was killed in battle with the Nobunaga clan in 1560 and Ieyasu seized the opportunity to escape and return to his family lands in Mikawa. He made an alliance with the Nobunaga family, changing his name to Tokugawa Ieyasu, and started building up a home power base and his army. Ieyasu gradually expanded his territory, taking some of Nobunaga's land on his death in 1582, and also grabbing former Imagawa lands. He moved his headquarters to Sumpu, the city where he had been held hostage, and by 1583 he was master of five provinces.

For a decade he lived in the uneasy shadow of Japan's dominant warlord, Nobunaga's successor Toyotomi Hideyoshi, and keeping in with him even managed to share in some of his spoils

A Test of Loyalty

■ Ieyasu was forced to kill his first wife and order his son's suicide as proof of loyalty to Nobunaga. This demonstration of the low value of human life compared with honor clearly had an impact on Ieyasu: he once had a prisoner executed because he had insulted him when he was a child.

■ In his foreign affairs role, Ieyasu welcomed the new European traders; but he remained deeply suspicious of the Christian missionaries, and in 1614 he banned them.

■ By the time of his death, Ieyasu had built the largest castle in the world at Edo—a sprawling network of moats, stone walls, barbicans, and warehouses.

■ The Shogun rule of Japan (1600–1868) is named the Edo period, after the Tokugawa capital Edo (Tokyo).

Chronology

1543	Born in Okazaki, Japan, January 31
1550	Sent as hostage to Imagawa family at Sumpu
1560	Imagawa killed, Ieyasu returns home
1586	Ieyasu establishes new headquarters at Sumpu
1600	Ieyasu triumphs in battle at Sekigahara
1603	Appointed Shogun
1605	Retires and passes title to his son
1616	Dies in Sumpu, June 1

when he took over part of the Hojo domains. These included the fishing village of Edo (modern Tokyo). Avoiding involvement in Hideyoshi's two disastrous military expeditions to Korea, Ieyasu built up a productive and well-governed state, and, by the time Hideyoshi died in 1598, Ieyasu had the largest and most efficient army and the best-run domains in Japan. There was a final clash between Hideyoshi's former lieutenants and Ieyasu in 1600 at Sekigahara, some 50 miles (80 km) northeast of Kyoto, in which Ieyasu's eastern army triumphed. He was now undisputed master of Japan.

Ieyasu was a great organizer and he now set about rearranging his domains, redistributing land, switching warlords round, and placing his most trusted vassals in control of central Japan.

The powerless but prestigious imperial court confirmed his position in 1603, appointing him Shogun.

He retired from the post two years later and the title passed to his son, Hidetada, thus establishing the Tokugawa hereditary right. But as elder statesman, he retained great personal authority, and direct responsibility for foreign affairs.

He also had unfinished business and, to be absolutely certain of his son's inheritance, in 1614 and 1615 he mobilized his armies for two final assaults on the Hideyoshi stronghold. He reduced their great castle at Osaka and butchered the last of the Toyotomi. He died in 1616, having secured his family's dynasty and lasting peace.

Charles V

Charles V (1500–58) was Europe's greatest ruler after Charlemagne. As Holy Roman Emperor and King of Spain, this Habsburg monarch ruled over the first empire "on which the sun never set"—in Europe, North Africa, Spanish America, and the Far East. His achievement was to hold this vast and disparate empire together for more than forty years against a rising tide of Protestant insurgency, French hostility, papal antagonism, and Islamic incursions.

Charles V inherited his Burgundian and Austrian kingdoms, and his drooping jaw, from his grandfather, the Habsburg Holy Roman Emperor Maximilian, and his Spanish empire from his deranged mother, Joanna, daughter of Spain's joint monarchs Ferdinand and Isabella. He was brought up by his aunt Margaret of Austria in what is now Belgium, and his tutor was Adrian of Utrecht, a theologian who later became pope.

He began his reign as Charles I of Spain in 1516, and from then on his life was one of almost ceaseless travel. He went to Spain for the first time in 1517, but had to leave two years later to be crowned King of Germany and Holy Roman Emperor-elect. But the problems of his reign had just begun; the Spanish rebelled against their foreign king and the German Protestants started fomenting trouble in northern Europe.

Charles responded harshly to the "Comuneros" rebels in Spain, but he was forced to be more pragmatic with the Protestants in Germany. His vision was to restore religious unity to Europe and, though initially he rejected Martin Luther's attempts to reform the Catholic Church, later he was forced to grant the Protestants some rights.

Territorial squabbles with France over Burgundy and Italy dominated much of Charles's reign, involving him in five wars. Charles's

> *"There are those who say I wish to rule the world, but my thoughts and deeds demonstrate the contrary"*

Chronology	
1500	Born in Ghent, February 24
1507	Crowned Duke of Burgundy
1516	Becomes King of Castile and Aragon
1517	Travels to Spain for first time
1518	Elected Holy Roman Emperor
1519	Revolt of "Comuneros" in Spain
1525	Francis I of France prisoner in Madrid
1527	Sack of Rome by imperial armies
1535	Capture of Tunis
1556	Abdicates, and retires to Spain
1558	Dies in Yuste, Spain, September 21

Spanish and German troops shocked Europe by marching on France's ally, Pope Clement VII, and sacking Rome in 1527. The Peace of Cambrai in 1529 brought compromise: Charles gave up claims to Burgundy, Francis I to Milan and Naples. Peace was made with the pope, who crowned Charles as Holy Roman Emperor in Bologna.

A resurgent Islamic Turkey, under Süleyman the Magnificent, posed a grave threat to Charles's empire in the east, and he took up the struggle against it on land and at sea. In the 1530s he dispatched an army to defend Vienna against a possible Turkish invasion, and he sent fleets to capture Tunis and Algiers.

Charles took special interest in Spain's South American possessions. A source of immense wealth, in his eyes they were a challenge to his Christian duty. He accepted the arguments of the Jesuit theologian Bartolomé de las Casas against slavery.

A Life in the Saddle

■ Charles V spent one out of every four days traveling during his forty-three-year reign. He went to Germany nine times, seven times to Spain, seven times to Italy, four times to France, and twice to England and Africa. He spent twelve years in the Netherlands. He said, "My life has been one long journey."

■ Charles was also a great patron of the arts. He commissioned many portraits from the Italian artist Titian, who was duly created Count Palatine and a Knight of the Golden Spur. One day when in Titian's studio, Charles bent down to pick up his brushes from the floor—an extraordinary gesture for a monarch at that time.

■ Charles said, "There are those who say I wish to rule the world, but both my thoughts and my deeds demonstrate the contrary."

Charles tried to ensure his succession by preparing for his son Philip to marry Mary I of England, but the English refused to crown Philip, and Mary was childless. In 1555, in a moving speech in Brussels, Charles announced his decision to abdicate and give his lands in the Netherlands, Spain, and the Indies to his son Philip, and the imperial crown to his brother Ferdinand. His attempts at universal unity had failed. The empire he had held together for more than four decades was broken up. Suffering from gout and insomnia, he left for Spain accompanied by two of his sisters, and died in his palace at Yuste in Extremadura in western Spain in 1558.

Philip II

Philip II (1527–98), King of Spain, ruled over the first global empire: his dominions stretched from Europe to the Americas to the Far East. He had a genius for bureaucracy and was said to have governed his empire from "two inches of paper."

Philip II was the eldest son of the Holy Roman Emperor and King of Spain, Charles V, and his wife, Isabella of Portugal. His father was abroad for much of Philip's youth, and he was educated by tutors. He married four times. In 1543 he wed his cousin Maria of Portugal, and became de facto regent of Spain. Maria gave birth to a son Don Carlos, who was later accused of plotting against his father and who died in mysterious circumstances. His second wife was Mary Tudor, and Philip lived briefly as her consort in England.

By the time of his father Charles V's abdication in 1556, Philip was already Duke of Milan, King of Naples and Sicily, ruler of the Netherlands, and he was soon to inherit lands in the Americas and the Far East.

He fought in the battle of Saint Quentin against the French in 1557, achieving a victory which paved the way for the Treaty of Cateau Cambrésis in 1559 that ended sixty years of war with France. Philip then married for the third time to Elizabeth of Valois of France. They had two dearly

loved daughters, Isabella (who later became joint Governor of the Netherlands with her husband) and Catalina. His fourth marriage in 1570 was to his Austrian cousin, Anna, who gave birth to the future Philip III.

Philip was in the vanguard of the Catholic Church's attempt to regain its ascendancy after the Protestant Reformation; he was fanatically Catholic, and the Inquisition was his principal weapon. His harsh repression of rebellion in the Netherlands sparked an eighty-year war, which resulted in a split between the northern (Protestant) Netherlands, and the southern (Catholic) Belgium. In Spain, Philip's religious orthodoxy led him to oppress Christianized Moors (Moriscos). Many thousands were exiled after 1571.

Philip's palace complex at El Escorial was described as the "Eighth Wonder of the World"

Philip took the war against infidels to the Mediterranean where his half brother, Don John of Austria, led a Christian alliance to victory over the Ottoman Turks at the naval battle of Lepanto. Religion underpinned his decision to send his "Invincible Armada" to unseat Queen Elizabeth I in 1588, and return England to Catholicism, but the great fleet was scattered and destroyed by

A Bibliophile King

■ Philip was a collector: he owned thousands of coins and medals, precious stones, and arms and armor. He left more than 10,000 books in the library at El Escorial, and thousands of holy relics, including a supposed hair from Christ's beard, and the bodies of several early Christian martyrs.

■ Philip governed his global dominions from the center of Spain in Castile. Distrusting his advisers and secretaries, he insisted all important decisions be referred to him.

■ His youthful trips to northern Europe led him to create Flemish gardens for his palaces near Madrid and Segovia; many of his imported plants and trees died because his Spanish gardeners forgot to irrigate them.

■ El Escorial was regarded as the "eighth wonder of the world" by contemporaries, and by Philip as "the lady of his heart."

■ The Philippines, conquered in 1566, are named after Philip II.

violent storms. Philip also came to the aid of the Catholic Holy League in France, which was fighting the Huguenot (Protestant) King Henri IV from 1590 until 1598. He claimed his rights to the throne of Portugal in 1580.

For all his war-making, Philip was a tender, loving father and husband. While in Lisbon, pursuing his claim to the Portuguese throne in 1580, he wrote delightful letters to his daughters. Philip loved art, and like his father was a patron of Titian. He also developed a passion for the ghoulish work of Dutch master Hieronymus Bosch, but he found the originality of El Greco too much. He built and expanded palaces around Madrid. His major artistic achievement was the construction of El Escorial (1563–84), a monastery, palace, and royal mausoleum filled with paintings, books, and holy relics. Philip died peacefully in his bedchamber at El Escorial, clasping his father's crucifix, looking on to the High Altar of the church.

Chronology

1527	Born in Valladolid, Spain, May 21
1543	First of four marriages
1549–51	First trip to Italy and Netherlands
1553–9	Second trip to northern Europe and England
1559	Treaty of Cateau Cambrésis with France
1563	Monastery palace of El Escorial begun
1568	Revolt of the Netherlands begins
1571	Ottoman Turks defeated at Lepanto
1580	Conquers Portugal
1588	Sends "Armada" fleet to fight against England
1598	Dies at El Escorial, Spain, September 13

Elizabeth I

Elizabeth I (1533–1603), Queen of England, is widely regarded as the greatest of Britain's monarchs, who brought stability to the country after the tumult of previous reigns and who laid the political foundations of the English-speaking world.

Elizabeth was the only child of the marriage of Henry VIII to Anne Boleyn, from whom he had hoped for a male heir. For the sake of this marriage, he had divorced Catherine of Aragon and split with Rome. Anne Boleyn was, in her turn, executed. Henry then married Jane Seymour, who gave him a son, the future Edward VI. Princess Elizabeth received a superb humanist education, but her position at court was often fraught. During the reign of her brother Edward VI she became entangled with the over-

Chronology

1533	Born at Greenwich Palace on September 7
1554	Imprisoned in the Tower of London by her half sister Queen Mary
1558	Ascends throne on Mary's death
1568	Her cousin Mary Queen of Scots flees to England
1570	Excommunicated by Pope Pius V
1584	Sir Walter Raleigh granted a patent for colonizing America
1587	Mary Queen of Scots executed
1588	Defeat of the Spanish Armada
1601	Her favorite the Earl of Essex rebels and is executed
1603	Dies at Richmond, March 24

The Elizabethan Age

■ Elizabeth was extremely erudite and a brilliant linguist, and Elizabethan England has come to be seen as a golden age. But she showed little interest in drama, and in fact most of Shakespeare's plays were written after her death.

■ The popular image is of Elizabeth gleefully ordering executions, but she never used execution as a tool of policy: only one of her servants was ever dismissed, and none executed, and she took years to decide to have Mary, Queen of Scots, executed.

■ Pope Sixtus V, sponsor of the Spanish Armada, said of her: "She certainly is a great Queen and were she only a Catholic she would be our dearly beloved. Just look how well she governs! She is only a woman, only mistress of half an island, and yet she makes herself feared by Spain, by France, by the Empire, by all.'

ambitious Lord Seymour, and during the reign of her half sister Mary she became the natural rallying-point of Protestant opposition.

By the time she ascended the throne on November 17, 1558, Elizabeth had acquired a thorough knowledge of statecraft, guided from the beginning by her adviser Sir William Cecil, later Lord Burghley. Her first and perhaps longest-lasting achievement was the establishment of the Church of England, alienating Roman Catholics, who had a champion in her cousin the Catholic Mary Queen of Scots (mother of her successor James I), while her moderation made her unpopular with the more earnest Protestant brethren.

Cecil apart, the dominating figure early in her reign was Lord Robert Dudley, whom she created Earl of Leicester and who was, it seems, the real love of her life. But Leicester had been accused of murdering his wife and was an unsuitable match; and so, throughout the first decades of her reign, Elizabeth conducted a

series of fantastically elaborate and protracted courtships with a string of foreign suitors, the most famous being the Duke of Alençon, brother of the French king. Later on, when it became plain that she would never marry, the cult of the Virgin Queen blossomed; and when Sir Walter Raleigh attempted to establish the first colony in America, it was named Virginia in her honor. It was these later years that have given us the archetype of the Virgin Queen surrounded by doting poet-courtiers. The last decade of her reign was dominated by the Earl of Essex, young enough to be her son; but this foundered when he attempted a rising in 1601 and was executed.

At home and abroad, Elizabeth's policy was characterized by caution, thrift, and a notable reluctance to squander human life. She gave reluctant support both to Henri IV, the Protestant King of France, and to the Protestants in the Netherlands, fighting against the rule of Philip II of Spain. At sea, she tolerated, and sometimes profited handsomely from, the exploits of privateers such as Sir Francis Drake. Eventually Philip II was goaded into launching the ill-fated Spanish Armada of 1588. It was on this occasion that Elizabeth made the speech that has come to define her both as a woman and as a ruler: "I know I have the body of a weak and feeble woman, but I have the heart and stomach of a king, and of a king of England too…"

The last decade of Elizabeth's reign was marked by something akin to a sense of weariness, brought about partly by an economic downturn, by a series of bad harvests, and by the ruinous expense of the English campaign to subdue Ireland.

"I know I have the body of a weak and feeble woman, but I have the heart of a King …"

33

Frederick the Great

Frederick the Great (1712–86), King of Prussia, waged war to expand his nation and make it a European power, and introduced liberal reforms at home, which earned him the title "enlightened despot."

Frederick was brought up in two contrasting worlds. He was constantly beaten by his father, King Frederick-William I, and was forced to watch the execution of his friend, Lieutenant Hans von Katte, with whom he had tried to escape to England; and was then imprisoned by his father. Encouraged by his mother, and in contrast to the strict Prussian military atmosphere of his father's household, Frederick had developed a taste for the arts and music and French literature. He corresponded with and met the leading French philosopher Voltaire, played the flute and wrote music and poetry, and he was homosexual; he also eventually applied himself to his father's business and became a brilliant soldier and administrator. And he was strong willed.

Within days of taking over from his father as King Frederick II, he plunged Prussia into war. He was determined to make use of the highly trained army he had inherited from his father, and for a quarter of a century war was his prime instrument of policy. The first target was Habsburg-ruled Silesia, which Frederick seized from Austria's new Empress Maria Theresa. He fought two wars for possession of these strategically rich mining and agricultural duchies, in 1740–42 and 1744–5. His first battle, Mollwitz, was a near disaster; he fled the field before his disciplined army won the day. But from then on Frederick notched up a string of impressive victories, often overwhelming far larger armies through bold offensive action. The flute-playing intellectual had grown into a brilliant military campaigner.

In 1756, King Frederick launched a new war by invading Saxony, a move that historians liken to Germany's preemptive strikes in the European wars of the twentieth century. Frederick's justification was that he was encircled and threatened, that he had to attack to survive. The invasion pitted Frederick's Prussia against the armies of Austria, Russia, Sweden, Saxony, and France, and dragged Europe into the Seven Years War. Frederick won most but not all the battles, and came out on top, if only by the skin of his teeth, thanks in large part to the timely death in 1762 of his arch-enemy, Empress Elizabeth of Russia. He had gained no new territory and exhausted his army and state, but he had emerged with a reputation for military greatness. Aided only by the British Treasury, he had established Prussia as the leading rival to Austria for the domination of German Europe, and in the diplomatic maneuvering following the war he carved up Poland with Russia in 1772, and gained Polish Prussia and Torún. In 1779, he grabbed more land from Austria, the Franconian principalities of Bavaria. In the end he tripled

> *"My people and I have come to an agreement ... They are to say as they please, and I am to do as I please"*

Chronology

1712	Born in Berlin, January 24
1730	Imprisoned by his father in Küstrin fortress
1740	Accedes to the throne as King Frederick II
1741	First victory, at Mollwitz
1756	Invades Saxony
1759	Defeated by Russia at Battle of Kunersdorf
1763	Peace of Hubertusburg ends Seven Years War
1772	First partition of Poland
1786	Dies at Sans Souci, August 17

Kingship and the State

Frederick the Great's writing fills thirty volumes. In this tract written in 1752, he sets out his views of kingship and government:

■ "Politics is the science of always using the most convenient means in accord with one's own interests."

■ "A well-conducted government must have an underlying concept so well integrated that it could be likened to a system of philosophy. All actions taken must be well reasoned, and all financial, political, and military matters must flow toward one goal, which is the strengthening of the state and the furthering of its power."

■ "The sovereign is the first servant of the state."

■ "Catholics, Lutherans, Reformed, Jews, and other Christian sects live in this state, and live together in peace…It is of no concern in politics whether the ruler has a religion or whether he has none. All religions, if one examines them, are founded on superstition, more or less absurd. It is impossible for a man of good sense, who dissects their contents, not to see their error; but these prejudices, these errors and mysteries, were made for men, and one must know enough to respect the public and not to outrage its faith, whatever religion is involved."

Prussia's population and almost doubled its territory.

At home, he was an absolute ruler, but he also embraced the principles of the Enlightenment and exercised a large degree of tolerance, allowing a free press, freedom of speech, and freedom of religion. "My people and I have come to an agreement which satisfies us both," he once remarked. "They are to say as they please, and I am to do as I please."

Frederick continued the work of his predecessors in modernizing the Prussian state administration. He issued a new code of Prussian law, the *Codex Fridericanus*, made judges sit stiff exams, outlawed torture and curtailed the death sentence, but, fearful of the reaction of his powerful Junker landlords, he stopped short of abolishing serfdom. The king also patronized the arts and encouraged science and learning, laying the groundwork for universal primary education. But in the end it was the army that counted in Frederick's Prussia: it took 50 percent of the state budget and increased from 80,000 to 190,000 in the course of his reign. Frederick died in 1786 at Sans Souci, the rococo palace he built near Berlin.

George Washington

George Washington (1732–99) commanded the army of America's rebel colonies fighting for independence from Great Britain and became the first President of the United States.

Born in Virginia in 1732, the son of a tobacco farmer and grandson of an immigrant from Northamptonshire, England, George Washington wanted to be rich and successful, but was destined for much greater things. With more ambition than formal education, he became a skillful surveyor and avid land speculator. Initially modeling himself on his cultured older half brother, Lawrence, who had married into Virginia's elite, Washington succeeded to his Mount Vernon estate following Lawrence's early death from TB. Militia service brought Washington further social advancement and invaluable experience in fortification, finance, and frontier diplomacy. Retiring from active service at twenty-seven to marry a wealthy widow, Martha Custis (1731–1802), the slave-owning squire then busied himself with estate improvement and the Virginia House of Burgesses. British attempts to limit land acquisition in the interests of frontier security caused Washington much personal aggravation, embroiling him in opposition politics. The outbreak of the revolutionary war brought him command of the rebel army, partly in deference to his previous military experience, partly in recognition of the need to bind Virginia to the rebel cause.

As a general, Washington proved a dogged survivor of defeats rather than an architect of victories. No military genius but an excellent administrator, he held together a patchwork force of fractious patriots despite chronic

An "English" Gentleman

■ Ironically, the father of the great republic epitomized the qualities of an English country gentleman, reluctant for office but dutiful in its performance, jealous of personal honor but indifferent to public regard, more content on his broad acres than in the counsels of power. Fittingly, the Stars and Stripes flag that symbolized the independence of his country is based on the heraldic coat of arms of his English ancestors.

■ Washington's iconic stature as the personification of American virtue was rapidly enhanced by the appearance of Mason Locke Weems's *Life and Memorable Actions of George Washington* (1806), which first circulated the legend of the cherry tree. Subsequent biographers of note included Washington Irving (1855–9) and future President Woodrow Wilson (1896).

■ Thomas Paine, who had served in Washington's army, dedicated his Rights of Man to him, but said that he was "treacherous in private friendship...and a hypocrite in public life."

■ Historian Samuel Eliot Morison summarized Washington's career as that of "a simple gentleman of Virginia who so disciplined himself that he could lead an insubordinate and divided people into ordered liberty and enduring union."

Washington's success in the terrible winter at Valley Forge proved vital to the final American victory

shortages of supply and arms and recurrent uncertainties of support from the Continental Congress and state governments. Successfully forcing the British from Boston, he abandoned New York adroitly to regroup at White Plains and gain tactical successes at Trenton and Princeton, which proved vital in lifting morale and acquiring much-needed stores. Following major defeats at Brandywine and Germantown, Washington's success in simply maintaining his force through a terrible winter at Valley Forge in 1777–8 proved crucial to final victory, but thereafter his command was limited to strategic direction, as campaigning in the south took priority and the intervention of French forces finally proved decisive in defeating the divided commands of the British. In September 1781 Washington left his New York headquarters to assume personal command of the Franco-American forces, which successfully forced the surrender of the besieged British at Yorktown, effectively ending the war.

Denied a longed-for rural retirement, Washington was pestered into serving as president, first of the constitutional convention of 1787 and then of the new nation itself. As such he established an efficient civil service and financial stability. Reelected to a second

Chronology

1732	Born at Wakefield, Westmoreland County, February 22
1755–9	Commands Virginia Regiment
1775–83	Commander in Chief of the Continental Army
1789–97	Serves as first President of the United States
1799	Dies at Mount Vernon, Virginia, December 14

term of office, in 1794 Washington also assumed personal command in suppressing the "Whiskey Rebellion" against the taxing powers of the Federal government. When war broke out between Britain and France, he maintained U.S. neutrality against pro-French pressures from Thomas Jefferson and his supporters. Emerging factionalism at home made Washington grateful to decline a third presidential term, thus establishing a convention that endured until Franklin D. Roosevelt won four terms.

Washington explained this decision in a farewell presidential address (another precedent) deploring the growth of political parties and warning against entanglements in foreign affairs. Returning briefly to nominal command when war threatened with France in 1798–99, Washington died on December 14, 1799 at Mount Vernon and was buried there. When news of his death reached England, his old enemies honored him with a 20-gun salute fired by the Channel fleet.

Abraham Lincoln

Abraham Lincoln (1809–65) was the 16th President of the United States. Although he was responsible for the abolition of slavery, Lincoln pursued the bloodiest conflict in American history not to right an historic wrong, but to preserve an historic principle, the unity of a nation.

Although few burnished Lincoln's legend more assiduously than Lincoln himself, he really was born in a log cabin and really was almost entirely self-educated. After qualifying as a lawyer, he entered politics as a Whig in the Illinois legislature (1834–41) before moving up to Congress (1847–9), where he proposed a bill for the gradual and compensated emancipation of slaves.

Abandoning politics for a thriving legal practice, Lincoln returned to the fray when the Kansas–Nebraska Act (1854) opened western territories to slavery. Entrusting his fortunes to the new Republican Party, Lincoln established a national reputation in 1858 through debating the slavery issue with Stephen A. Douglas, his

Chronology

1809	Born Hodgenville, Kentucky, February 12
1834	Enters Illinois state legislature
1847–9	As Congressman opposes Mexican War and proposes emancipation
1858	Lincoln–Douglas debates
1860	Elected President
1863	January First Emancipation Proclamation comes into force
1864	Reelected President
1865	April 9, Robert E. Lee surrenders at Appomattox Courthouse, Va. April 15, Lincoln assassinated by actor John Wilkes Booth at Ford's Theater, Washington, DC

Democratic (and successful) opponent for the U.S. Senate. In 1860 he attained the presidency in a four-way contest, gaining only 39 percent of the popular vote. By the time he succeeded to office, seven southern states had already seceded from the Union to form the Confederacy. Lincoln used his inaugural address to pledge acceptance of slavery where it already existed but also to confirm his determination to uphold the solidarity of the Union. Four more states then seceded, but Lincoln retained the loyalty of a further four potential recruits to the rebellion.

Although possessed of far greater industrial and manpower resources than the Confederacy, Lincoln was initially hampered in his prosecution of the war by inadequate generals. However, when George B. McClellan (1826–86) failed to pursue Robert E. Lee after defeating his incursion northward at Antietam in September 1862, Lincoln capitalized on this limited success to issue the Emancipation Proclamation, which freed slaves

After Ulysses S. Grant took Vicksburg, splitting Confederate forces in the West, Lincoln appointed him to supreme command. Grant delegated the western campaign to Sherman, set Sheridan on a hugely destructive raid through Georgia, and himself enveloped Lee's forces in Virginia, although unable to rout him decisively in the field. However, Union successes proved sufficient to secure Lincoln's reelection in 1864 with 55 percent of the vote.

Lincoln's Address

Lincoln's speech at the dedication of the Gettysburg National Assembly on November 19 1863 followed a two-hour oration by Edward Everett, one of the most famous speakers of the time. "I wish that I could flatter myself that I had come as near to the central idea in two hours as you did in two minutes," Everett wrote afterward to Lincoln.

The Gettysburg Address

■ "Four score and seven years ago our fathers brought forth on this continent, a new nation, conceived in Liberty, and dedicated to the proposition that all men are created equal.

■ "Now we are engaged in a great civil war, testing whether that nation or any nation so conceived and so dedicated, can long endure. We are met on a great battlefield of that war. We have come to dedicate a portion of that field as a final resting place for those who here gave their lives that that nation might live. It is altogether fitting and proper that we should do this.

■ "But, in a larger sense, we cannot dedicate—we cannot consecrate—we cannot hallow—this ground. The brave men, living and dead, who struggled here, have consecrated it, far above our poor power to add or detract. The world will little note, nor long remember what we say here, but it can never forget what they did here. It is for us the living, rather, to be dedicated here to the unfinished work which they who fought here have thus far so nobly advanced. It is rather for us to be here dedicated to the great task remaining before us—that from these honored dead we take increased devotion to that cause for which they gave the last full measure of devotion—that we here highly resolve that these dead shall not have died in vain—that this nation, under God, shall have a new birth of freedom—and that government of the people, by the people, for the people, shall not perish from the Earth."

"That government of the people, by the people, for the people, shall not perish from the Earth"

Lincoln's far-sighted vision for the postwar reconstruction of a defeated South, sketched in his masterly

in rebel areas and welcomed freedmen into military service. Slavery ended officially with the Thirteenth Amendment in 1865.

Following further defeats at Fredericksburg and Chancellorsville, the Union finally prevailed in repulsing a second Confederate advance at Gettysburg in July 1863. The brief but brilliant valedictory address proclaimed there by Lincoln on November 19 that same year was subsequently hailed as a milestone of American oratory, but was inaudible to many and scarcely mentioned in the press coverage of the event.

second inaugural address ("With malice toward none, with charity for all…"), proved too lenient for a vengeful Congress, but the issue remained unresolved when an assassin's hand struck down the president within a week of Lee's surrender.

Gifted with humor and eloquence, Lincoln was criticized in his lifetime as wily, calculating, vacillating, and a demagogue—"fox populi" as *Vanity Fair* put it in 1863. To become president he had sometimes to sound more radical than he was; to survive as president he was compelled to act more cautiously than he might have wished.

Victoria

Queen Victoria (1819–1901) presided for sixty-three years over a glittering and expanding empire. Although as constitutional monarch she had no formal power, she gave her name to an age, and was one of the best-known figures in the world in the nineteenth century.

Princess Victoria was the daughter of George IV's brother, Prince Edward, Duke of Kent, and Princess Victoria of Saxe-Coburg. After the death of her father, Victoria was closely brought up by her mother, who dreamed of power through her daughter, but almost the first thing that Victoria did on her accession at just eighteen was to assert her own authority and independence.

Though she believed it was a job no woman should hold, the young queen set out to take an active part in ruling her country, and she learned her role from her elderly, conservative-minded Prime Minister, Lord Melbourne, a Whig, whom she "loved like a father." When his government fell to the Tories, she precipitated a serious constitutional crisis by refusing to appoint Tory ladies to her household. Melbourne's influence waned when Victoria married her first cousin Prince Albert of Saxe-Coburg-Gotha. It was a passionate love match, at least on Victoria's side, and together they set an unprecedented example of sedate, respectable, royal family life. They had four sons and five daughters.

Queen Victoria combined the roles of monarch and matriarch with a great zest for life

Victoria was at her most active as a ruler in collaboration with her "beloved Albert." She ardently supported all his projects, from the rebuilding of their homes, Osborne House on the Isle of Wight and Balmoral in Scotland, to the resounding success of the Great Exhibition, held at the Crystal Palace in 1851.

The diminutive Victoria was blessed with a robust constitution, but not Albert; the shock of his death at the age of forty-two in 1861 drove the queen, as passionate in grief as in love, into deep seclusion for many years. An iron sense of duty kept her involved privately in overseeing the business of government but she neglected her public royal duties, such as the Opening of Parliament, and grew very unpopular. One of the few people she allowed near her was, famously, a Scottish servant, John Brown, who treated her with a brusque, comforting directness. Speculation flourished on the nature of the friendship, probably because it cut across accepted norms.

Her popularity returned as she emerged from seclusion, encouraged by her Prime Minister Benjamin Disraeli, whom she preferred to his predecessor William Gladstone (because, said Disraeli, Gladstone treated her less like a woman and more like a government department). In 1876, Disraeli persuaded Parliament to proclaim Victoria Empress of India and, with her Golden and Diamond Jubilees, this small, dumpy, revered figure dressed in black became a symbol of imperial power, and regained her popularity.

Queen Victoria combined the figure of monarch and matriarch, and she had a great zest for life. In Albert's day she danced, traveled by the new railways in Germany and France, and

Chronology

1819	Born in Kensington Palace, London, May 24
1837	Succeeds to throne, June 20
1838	Crowned
1840	Marries Prince Albert, February 10
1861	Prince Albert dies, December 14
1876	Declared Empress of India
1887	Golden Jubilee
1897	Diamond Jubilee
1901	Dies at Osborne House, Isle of Wight, January 22

reveled in their holidays together at Osborne and Balmoral. An acute and interested observer, she recorded everything in her journal, parts of which were published as *Leaves from the Journal of my Life in the Highlands*. Her sketchbooks were filled with little watercolors of her children and her favorite views. In later life, she frequently traveled to Europe, but she never visited India.

Queen Victoria was truthful, strong-willed, stubborn, emotional, tough, commonsensical, uncompromising, shy, hot-tempered, rich in contradictions, headstrong, and alone: after Albert, there was no one on level terms who could truly help and advise her. This makes her transition into a legendary queen, who gave her name to an age, all the more remarkable.

This longest-reigning of British monarchs died at Osborne House on January 20 beneath the photograph of Albert on his deathbed which had been pinned to the bedhead forty years before, and was succeeded by her son, Edward VII.

Victoria's Legacy

■ Victoria's children and grandchildren married far and wide into the royal houses of Europe, with important diplomatic and dynastic implications. Her eldest daughter, Victoria, was married to the German heir in the hopes of steering Germany in a liberal direction, an intent thwarted through personalities, illness, and death.

■ Queen Victoria's most catastrophic legacy was the transmission of her hemophiliac gene to the Romanovs.

■ The famous "we are not amused" statement reputedly arose from her stern reaction to a joke told to her by some of her grandchildren.

Otto von Bismarck

Prince Otto von Bismarck (1815–98) was a Prusso-German statesman who used war and diplomacy to reunify Germany and become the first chancellor of the new German Empire. He was one of Europe's greatest nineteenth-century statesmen.

Bismarck was the son of a prosperous Prussian Junker landowner and a well-educated mother. He studied law in Göttingen and Berlin, leaving an account of himself as a dueler and drinker, and entered government service in 1836. But he resigned soon after to look after his estates and came back to Berlin in 1847 as a delegate to Prussia's United Diet (Parliament). He first made his mark in politics as a trenchant landowning conservative during the nationalist liberal revolutions that swept Europe in 1848, fanned by demands for greater democracy and self-rule. Three years later, in 1851, Bismarck came face to face with the realities of nationalism when he was posted to Frankfurt to represent Prussia at the German Confederation, a league of the thirty-nine German states. They were all divided: some under the sway of Prussia, most in the south dominated by Austria, which he began to think of as a "wormy old warship." It was Bismarck's achievement to exploit the conditions that made it possible to unite these disparate states into a unified Germany, under Prussian and not Austrian control.

Bismarck moved to St Petersburg in 1859 as ambassador to Russia, and then to Paris for a few brief summer months in 1862 as ambassador to France. Conservative landlord, soldier, lawyer, government servant, and ambassador, he was perfectly placed when a dispute broke out between the Prussian Parliament and King William I over military budgets, which Parliament wanted to reduce. The king would not agree. Bismarck was recalled from Paris and named prime minister and foreign minister in 1862, and broke the deadlock by continuing to apply the old budget.

"The great questions of the time are not decided by speeches and majority decisions," he said, "but by iron and blood."

Over the next ten years, Germany was reunited in three lightning wars: in 1864 Bismarck attacked and defeated Denmark, and laid claim to the Danish duchies of Schleswig and Holstein. When Austria quarreled over these spoils in 1866, he attacked and defeated her and her German allies at Königgrätz, incorporated some southern German states, and set up a Prussian-led North German Confederation. The reality of growing Prusso-German power sent shockwaves through Europe, which Bismarck

> *"The great questions ... are not decided by speeches and majority decisions, but by iron and blood"*

Chronology

1815	Born at Schönhausen, near Berlin, April 1
1847	Enters politics as delegate to Prussia's Diet
1859	Ambassador to St Petersburg
1862	Ambassador to Paris
1862	Appointed Minister-President of Prussia
1864	Defeats Denmark, claims Schleswig and Holstein
1866	Defeats Austria, annexes southern German states
1870	Defeats France, annexes Alsace-Lorraine
1871	German Empire declared, Bismarck Chancellor
1890	Dismissed from office
1898	Dies at his estate near Hamburg, July 30

skillfully exploited by tricking Louis Napoleon into war against the German states. When the French Emperor, outraged he had not been ceded Luxembourg and that a German prince had been offered the Spanish throne, made bellicose noises, Bismarck invaded France in 1870, and won a decisive battle at Sedan. In the euphoria of victory, the southern German states joined a united Germany, and the following year, in 1871, the new German Empire was proclaimed in the Palace of Versailles. Germany annexed Alsace-Lorraine and exacted a five-billion franc indemnity from France—sanctions the French would not forget.

Bismarck governed Germany as an autocratic chancellor for the next two decades. He applied the same tactics to domestic policy as he had to the maps of Europe. With no party power base to support him, he demanded absolute loyalty and, when he did not get it, he waged war: first against the Catholics on whom he imposed financial penalties and onerous burdens, and then against the Poles and the Socialists. He outlawed the Social Democratic Party and, fearful of revolution, he tried to outflank them by introducing accident and health insurance and pensions. He bribed and bludgeoned the press. Abroad, he pursued a largely cautious and peaceful foreign policy, based on interlocking alliances, which kept the European peace for more than half a century but which were ultimately to prove fatal for all parties in World War I.

Like many great leaders, Bismarck was a man of contradictions: a landlord who industrialized Germany; a conservative who gave Germany both universal male suffrage and social security; a monarchist who despised his emperor; a victor in wars who knew all too well the limitations of military power; a blustering, fearsome man in public beset by hysteria and insomnia in private, keeping himself going in later years on morphine.

After he was dismissed by Emperor William II, Bismarck retired to his estate near Hamburg, where he died in 1898.

The Iron Chancellor

■ Bismarck came to be known as the Iron Chancellor because of his use of the phrase "blood and iron" in speeches, although they were about budgets, not wars.
■ "You can do everything with bayonets," he said, "except sit on them."
■ Bismarck knew the limitations of power: he did not seek to "control the current of events, only occasionally to deflect it." He was a master of the limited war.

Winston Churchill

Soldier, journalist, historian, painter, Nobel-prize winning author, and politician, Sir Winston Churchill (1874–1965) gambled with destiny and led Britain through the darkest days of World War II to eventual victory over Nazi Germany.

Born in Blenheim Palace, the seat of his ancestor the Duke of Marlborough, Churchill was the son of a prominent Tory politician and an American heiress. He was educated at Harrow and trained as an army officer at Sandhurst. He saw action in two colonial spats, on the Northwest Frontier and in Sudan, and began writing about his exploits; *The Story of the Malakand Field Force* was the first of fifteen books. Leaving the army, he reported the Boer War for the *Morning Post*, further enhancing his reputation when he was captured and escaped.

In 1900 he was elected Conservative Member of Parliament for Oldham, but he lost faith in the Conservatives over free trade, and joined the Liberals. With meticulous preparation and endless rehearsal, Churchill mastered a speech impediment and developed into a skilled and effective orator.

He entered Cabinet in 1908 as President of the Board of Trade, one of several ministerial posts he held before and during World War I. As First Lord of the Admiralty from 1911, he pushed hard to build new battleships to match Germany. In 1915 he was held responsible for the abortive naval attack on the Dardanelles and the bungled landings in Gallipoli. He resigned and left for France to fight in the trenches. In 1917, he was recalled to office by Lloyd George as Minister for Munitions, where he threw himself behind the roll-out of the new battle-winning tank, and from 1919 to 1920 as Secretary of State for War, when he supported the Allied campaign in Russia against the Bolsheviks. As Colonial Secretary from 1921 to 1922, he ordered mass bombings of rebel Iraqis and even

"Never in the field of human conflict was so much owed by so many to so few"

Quotes

Among his famous sayings:

■ We shall fight on the beaches, we shall fight on the landing grounds, we shall fight in the fields and in the streets, we shall fight in the hills; we shall never surrender." June 4, 1940.

■ "Never was so much owed by so many to so few." About the pilots who fought in the Battle of Britain.

■ Accused by a hostile lady of being drunk at dinner, he replied: "And you, madam, are ugly, but I shall be sober tomorrow."

■ Nancy Astor told him: "Winston, if I were your wife I would put poison in your coffee," to which Churchill replied: "If you were my wife, I would drink it."

proposed using chemical weapons against them. In 1924 he became Chancellor of the Exchequer in a Conservative government, and exacerbated his already poor relations with the trade unions by helping to break the 1926 General Strike.

For most of the next decade, Churchill was in the political wilderness, increasingly isolated as he warned of the rising threat of Nazi Germany; few would listen. He also alienated people over his support for the king in the abdication crisis and by his opposition to Indian nationalists. His hour came when war broke out. Brought back to head the Admiralty, where he managed to avoid blame for the failure in Norway, he was called to replace the discredited Neville Chamberlain as Prime Minister in May 1940. "I felt as if I were walking with destiny," he said, "and that all my

dressed in a boiler suit and giving his trademark "V" salute—he mobilized and inspired an entire nation. Once America joined the war and President Roosevelt started to take center stage, with Russia's Stalin, in shaping the final victory and the postwar world, Churchill began to fade from the picture. He was attending the last "Big Three" summit in Potsdam when he was voted out of office.

Churchill remained a challenging if bored opposition leader but, in his "Iron Curtain" speech in Fulton, Missouri, in 1946, he used his position as a world statesman to masterful effect when he warned of the growing Soviet threat. He had a final stint as Prime Minister in 1951 but illness, following a series of strokes, forced him to resign in 1955.

Churchill retired to Chartwell, his country house in Kent, and spent his last years writing, painting, and taking vacations. In his lifetime he was seen as the greatest living Englishman, a reputation that has declined little since his death in 1965.

past life had been but a preparation for this hour and this trial."

In fact he gambled with destiny. With continental Europe in Hitler's grasp, Churchill took an enormous risk and chose to fight on alone in 1940, without knowing that the following year Japan would attack Pearl Harbor and that Germany would declare war on the United States—events that ensured America would once again come to the rescue.

His unflinching determination in the face of the Axis powers during the Blitz and the Battle of Britain won massive support. He promised nothing more than "blood, toil, tears, and sweat," but through his speeches to Parliament, his radio broadcasts, and his public displays of defiance—scrambling over bombed-out sites

Chronology

1874	Born in Blenheim Palace, Oxfordshire, November 30
1895	Leaves Sandhurst as cavalry officer
1897	Action on Northwest Frontier
1899	Reports Boer War, captured and escapes
1900	First elected to Parliament
1908	President of Board of Trade
1910–11	Home Secretary
1911–15	First Lord of the Admiralty
1919–20	Secretary of State for War
1924	Chancellor of Exchequer
1940	Prime Minister
1945	Loses postwar general election
1951–5	Prime Minister
1963	Made honorary United States citizen
1965	Dies in London, January 24

Charles de Gaulle

General Charles de Gaulle (1890–1970) was a military leader and statesman who led France through two major crises—World War II and defeat of Nazi Germany, and the birth of the Fifth French Republic and independence of Algeria.

Born Charles André Joseph Marie de Gaulle in Lille, northern France, he grew up in Paris where his father worked as a teacher at a Jesuit school. Graduating from Saint-Cyr military academy, he fought in World War I at Verdun and was wounded three times and three times mentioned in dispatches. He was captured by the Germans in 1916, and spent two and a half years as a prisoner of war, attempting to escape five times.

After the war, and in between teaching and further training at the War College, he was sent on missions to Poland, the Rhineland, and the Middle East. On promotion to lieutenant colonel, he joined the National Defense Council. He wrote books and articles on military subjects, displaying talent as both a writer and a thinker. In *The Army of the Future* (1934) he criticized France's reliance on the static Maginot line for defense against Germany, calling instead for a small, highly mechanized mobile army. He was delivering the same message to politicians as late as January 1940, but his advice went unheeded, and, in May and June 1940, Nazi German forces swiftly and easily overran France.

"One can't impose unity out of the blue on a country that has 265 different kinds of cheese."

De Gaulle was commanding a tank brigade at the outbreak of war, and on June 6, 1940, now a temporary brigadier general, he was called into the beleaguered government as Under-Secretary of State for Defense. When Marshal Pétain took over ten days later with the intention of suing for peace, de Gaulle moved to London and, on June 18, 1940, he announced the formation of a French government in exile. He became head of the French Committee for National Liberation,

the body that directed the Free French Movement, but was sentenced to death in his absence by a French military court. At first he plowed a lonely furrow; he was unknown and had no political status. But he had absolute belief in his mission and obstinate determination. His relations with the British were never easy, and in 1943 he moved his headquarters to Algiers.

De Gaulle was given a hero's welcome on his return to Paris in August 1944 in the wake of the Allied Normandy landings. He assumed power as president of a provisional government, and guided France through the drafting of a new constitution. Seeking to avoid the political instability of the Third Republic, which had ended in the humiliating collapse of 1940, de Gaulle argued for a strong executive presidency and a subordinate parliament. When his wishes

Chronology

1890	Born in Lille, northern France, November 22
1913	Graduates from Saint-Cyr as 2nd lieutenant
1916	Wounded and captured at Verdun
1940	Appointed Under-Secretary of Defense
1940	De Gaulle escapes to London, issues call to French Resistance June 18
1943	Transfers headquarters to Algiers
1944	Triumphal return to Paris
1945	President of the provisional government
1958	Elected President of Fifth French Republic
1965	Elected President for second term
1969	Resigns after losing referendum on reform
1970	Dies, Colombey-les-Deux-Églises, November 9

were ignored, he resigned, but over the next decade he remained in the political limelight, as leader of the Rally of the French People, and he also wrote his memoirs.

As he had predicted, the Fourth Republic soon ran into trouble; by 1958 a revolt in French-held Algeria, combined with runaway inflation and financial instability at home, had brought France once again to the brink. There was real threat of civil war. De Gaulle came out of retirement, and this time he got his way. On December 21, 1958 he was elected President of the Fifth Republic under a new constitution that gives the president executive authority and which prevails today.

De Gaulle used the new presidential powers to face down a revolt by right-wing generals, determined to hang on to Algiers. He gave Algeria full independence in 1962 and unraveled France's remaining colonies. Egotistical and strongly nationalist, he set about strengthening France both financially and militarily. He developed France's own nuclear deterrent and withdrew French forces from NATO, and he famously vetoed the entry of pro-American Britain into the European Common Market. De Gaulle served two terms as president, ruling France like a general on a battlefield, with the referendum his mandate.

Quotes

■ De Gaulle was a master of the explosive short phrase.
■ In June 1940 de Gaulle proclaimed from London: "France has lost a battle. But France has not lost the war."
■ "Je vous ai compris," he told Algerians in June 1958. "I have understood you."
■ "Vive le Québec libre," he said in 1967 on the balcony of Montreal City Hall. "Long live Free Quebec." The statement caused a diplomatic uproar with Canada.
■ At home, de Gaulle could be equally diplomatic. "One can't impose unity ... on a country that has 265 different kinds of cheese," he once said.

Violent demonstrations by university students rocked France in 1968 and a general strike followed. De Gaulle responded by moving troops toward Paris, and by promising reform. A year later, de Gaulle resigned the presidency after losing a referendum on his reform proposals. He retired to Colombey-les-Deux-Églises, where he died from a heart attack in 1970.

Franklin D. Roosevelt

Franklin Delano Roosevelt (1882–1945), elected President of the United States four times, led the nation out of the Great Depression and through most of World War II. Patrician, controversial, and inconsistent, "FDR" transformed Federal government and paved the way for the United States to become a twentieth-century superpower.

Born to a wealthy family of Dutch origin on an estate overlooking the Hudson River, Roosevelt had a classic patrician East Coast education— Harvard University and Columbia Law School. After working briefly as a lawyer, he plunged into a political career, following in the footsteps of his fifth cousin, President Theodore Roosevelt—only as a Democrat. He was elected to the New York Senate in 1910, became Assistant Secretary to the Navy in 1913, and by 1920 he was Democratic nominee for Vice President.

That same year, aged thirty-nine, Roosevelt was stricken with poliomyelitis. He fought back to regain the use of his legs, particularly through swimming, but for the rest of his life he was confined to braces and wheelchairs.

In 1928 he became Governor of New York, and in November 1932, at the height of the Great Depression, in a contest of hope over despair, Roosevelt was elected President. He had offered confidence and a promise of action—a New Deal. "The only thing we have to fear," he said in his inaugural address, "is fear itself." When he took over there were 13 million unemployed and virtually every bank had closed its doors. Congress enacted a sweeping program to bring recovery to business and farming; the nation quit the gold standard, and millions were poured into

public works and emergency relief. Capitalist America even embarked on an experiment in public ownership in the Tennessee Valley hydro-electricity scheme. By the end of his first term, he had introduced social security, unemployment benefits, banking controls, higher taxes, and an end to prohibition. But despite renewed optimism, sustained recovery did not kick in until the economy went on to war footing in 1940.

Through the New Deal, Federal authorities significantly, and irreversibly, extended their power over American society. This mirrored what was happening in Europe and Russia, and although in America it was democratically implemented, conservatives claimed that Roosevelt had undermined rights of states and individual liberty. They also disliked the rise of organized labor.

Roosevelt was reelected in 1936 with an even larger majority and he set out to extend Federal authority by seeking to enlarge the Supreme Court, which had been blocking some of his New Deal. He lost the court battle but established the right of government to regulate the economy.

Roosevelt was a pragmatist in foreign policy. He pledged the United States to a "good neighbor" policy, a promise not to intervene in the internal affairs of countries in the region. He bowed to isolationism, conscious that most Americans blamed the Depression on their involvement in World War I, and he accordingly applied strict neutrality over Europe. He recognized the Soviet Union in 1933, and the United States at first did

A Way With Words

■ Roosevelt was one of the first politicians to exploit radio. He started broadcasting "fireside" chats as Governor of New York, and used radio to rally America during World War II. He began the custom of weekly presidential broadcasts.
■ He coined "The New Deal" at his nomination. "I pledge you, I pledge myself, to a new deal for the American people."
■ Roosevelt called the day of the attack on Pearl Harbor—December 7, 1941—"a date which will live in infamy."

little as Adolf Hitler grabbed power, unleashed war on Europe, and set about the mass extermination of Jews and Gypsies. When Poland, France, and Belgium fell to Hitler and Britain came under siege, Roosevelt, constrained by Congress, could provide only non-military assistance. He did eventually give substantial "non-neutral" aid to both Britain and Russia, including warships, but he won reelection in 1940 with a pledge that American boys would not fight foreign wars.

That changed when, on December 7, 1941, the Japanese attacked and nearly destroyed the U.S. Pacific fleet in Pearl Harbor. Roosevelt immediately geared the

"The only thing we have to fear is fear itself"

nation for global war, and he became one of the principal architects of the defeat of Germany and Japan, presiding over a sometimes strained alliance with Britain and Russia at a succession of international summits. He concentrated on shaping the postwar world through the embryonic United Nations, and in particular on drawing Soviet Russia into it. He saw Russia as a vital ally in the defeat of Fascism, but in the end he was duped by Soviet leader Joseph Stalin, who after the war imposed Communist dictatorship over half of eastern Europe. Elected for an unprecedented fourth term in 1944, Roosevelt died on April 12, 1945, less than a month before Nazi Germany surrendered.

Chronology

1882	Born in Hyde Park, New York, January 30
1903	Graduated Harvard
1907	Columbia Law School
1910	Elected to New York Senate
1913	Assistant Secretary to the Navy
1921	Stricken with polio
1928	Governor of New York
1932	Elected President for first term
1936	Elected for second term
1940	Elected for third term
1941	Pearl Harbor, U.S. enters World War II
1944	Wins unprecedented fourth term
1945	Dies in Warm Springs, Georgia, April 12

David Ben-Gurion

David Ben-Gurion (1886–1973) dedicated his life to establishing a Jewish homeland in Palestine, and was the first Prime Minister and founding father of Israel.

Born David Gruen in 1886 in Plonsk, then part of Russia and now in Poland, Ben-Gurion was educated in a Hebrew school founded by his father, a lawyer and ardent Zionist. Inheriting his father's passionate belief in the goal of a Jewish return to their original homeland, he became a teacher in a Warsaw Jewish school aged eighteen and joined a socialist-Zionist group, Poale Zion (Workers of Zion). Always learning and writing, he was a lifetime scholar.

In 1906, he emigrated to Palestine, which was then part of the Turkish-ruled Ottoman Empire; convinced that Jews had to start cultivating the land there again, he set up the first agricultural workers' commune, which evolved into the kibbutz movement. He also helped establish the Jewish self-defense movement, Hashomer (The Watchman), and became editor of the Hebrew-language newspaper *Achdut* (Unity). In Palestine, he adopted the surname Ben-Gurion, Hebrew for "son of the young lion."

He was deported to Egypt by the Turks in 1915, soon after the outbreak of of World War I, and traveled on behalf of the socialist-Zionist cause to New York, where he married a Russian émigré, Paula Munweis. When Britain took control of

Palestine from the crumbling Ottomans and issued the Balfour Declaration, which boosted Zionist hopes for a Jewish "national home," Ben-Gurion enlisted in the British army's Jewish Legion and rushed home to fight. But the war was over by the time he reached Palestine.

Under the British Mandate, he threw himself into labor union politics, founding in 1920 the Histadrut national confederation of Jewish workers. The Histadrut was effectively a "state within a state," and Ben-Gurion was the de facto local authority. Ten years later, Ben-Gurion founded the Israeli Workers Party and in 1935 he was elected executive chairman of the World Zionist Movement and head of the Jewish Agency in Palestine. Ben-Gurion cooperated with the British until 1939, but fell out with them when, yielding to Arab pressure, they started cutting back the flow of Jewish immigrants. From then on he was increasingly in the vanguard of the fight against the British, and after World War II he called openly for insurrection and authorized guerrilla attacks.

> *"What matters is not what the Gentiles say, but what the Jews do"*

It fell to Ben-Gurion to proclaim the State of Israel from the balcony of a Tel Aviv apartment in May 1948, and then to weld the underground forces into an army and lead the young nation as Prime Minister and Defense Minister through its first war with its Arab neighbors. The war was costly for both sides—1 percent of the Jewish population died as well as thousands of Arabs, and more than half a million Palestinians lost their homes. After the war, Ben-Gurion presided over the rapid development of the country—its kibbutz movement, the construction of new towns, the creation of a unified public education

Chronology

1886	Born Plonsk, Poland, October 16
1906	Emigrates to Palestine
1914	Deported by the Turks, travels to New York
1917	Returns to Palestine
1948	Becomes Prime Minister of Israel
1953	Quits government
1955	Prime Minister again
1963	Resigns
1970	Retires from political life
1973	Dies in Sde Boker, December 1

system, the establishment of a national water supply, the "greening" of the land, and the absorption of a huge influx of immigrants. During his thirteen years as premier, Israel's population tripled from half a million to 1.5 million.

He quit government in 1953 to live in his kibbutz home in Sde Boker, a pioneering settlement in the Negev Desert, but came back to government two years later, initially as Defense Minister and then again as Prime Minister. He led Israel through the 1956 Suez War, during which Israel joined Britain and France in their abortive invasion of Egypt, and briefly occupied the Sinai Peninsula.

Ben-Gurion resigned as Prime Minister in 1963, but remained active in politics until June 1970 as a member of the Knesset (Parliament) for splinter parties, which he founded. He retired for the last time to Sde Boker to write, and died there three years later in the shadow of the 1973 Yom Kippur War.

Architect of a Nation

■ Israeli poet Amos Oz said of him: "Part Washington, part Moses, he was the architect of a new nation state that altered the destiny of the Jewish people—and the Middle East."

■ Always a man of action, Ben-Gurion used to say: "What matters is not what the Gentiles say, but what the Jews do."

■ One of Ben-Gurion's most controversial acts as Prime Minister was to establish diplomatic relations with West Germany—a move bitterly contested at the time.

■ Ben-Gurion's home in Kibbutz Sde Boker, near Beersheba, was in the heart of the Negev Desert, which he loved. His house looked out over a dramatic desert landscape, and his tomb faces the same view.

Gamal Nasser

Gamal Abdel Nasser (1918–70) rose from humble origins to be the first President of Egypt. He nationalized the Suez Canal and became a hero of the Arab world, but his reputation suffered after he was defeated by Israel in 1967.

Gamal Abdel Nasser, the son of a postman, was born in a mud-brick house and raised in and around Alexandria and Cairo. After finishing his schooling in Cairo, he entered military college in 1936 and graduated two years later as an officer in the Egyptian army. Egypt was still under British rule, with a puppet, King Farouk, on the throne, and Nasser helped forge a clandestine nationalist group that sought independence—The Free Officers, El-Dhobatt El-Ahrar. He fought as a major in the first Arab–Israeli war in 1948, when neighboring Muslim countries tried, without success, to knock out the new Jewish state. Nasser was an officer in one of three battalions surrounded for weeks by the Israelis in a group of Arab villages called the Faluja Pocket.

Defeat in the war and general disaffection with the widespread corruption in government sparked an almost bloodless coup d'état in July 1952. Nasser was the leader, although he remained in the shadows for two more years. The rebel officers, nominally headed by General Mohammed Naguib, forced King Farouk to abdicate, and his son Ahmad Fuad was declared king in his place. The British agreed to pull out by 1954, but before that the army rebelled twice more—first to depose the young boy king and proclaim a republic under General Naguib, and then to depose Naguib and make Nasser head of state. He officially became president in 1956, and proclaimed Egypt an Arab socialist state, with Islam as the official religion.

Nasser now bared his nationalist teeth; Egypt unilaterally took over the Suez Canal, a vital waterway linking the Mediterranean and Arabian seas over which Britain had maintained control. Nasser nationalized the canal after Britain and the United States withdrew funding from his Aswan High Dam project. The move triggered a crisis, and the British and French, together with Israel, launched an air and ground invasion to retake the canal. The Americans, instinctively opposed to what they saw as the final fling of British imperialism, sided with Nasser and forced the invaders to pull back. British Prime Minister Anthony Eden resigned in humiliation. In the Arab world—and in other nations still ruled by European powers—Nasser was elevated to the status of a post-colonial hero, even though he

Charming and personable as an individual, as a politician Nasser ran a repressive police state

Damming the Nile

■ The Aswan High Dam was Nasser's most controversial legacy. Designed to harness the vast waters of the Upper Nile for hydropower and to irrigate thousands of acres of dry desert, it flooded many monuments that could not be rescued by UNESCO and had a damaging effect on the River Nile's water levels.

■ The 1956 Suez War still evokes strong emotions—but in retrospect, except in the context of the Cold War, it is hard to justify the armed intervention.

■ The scars of the 1967 war are still visible in the Sinai Desert—the burnt hulks of Egyptian tanks litter the landscape.

had lost part of the Sinai to Israel and had been blooded in the fighting. Egypt's takeover of the Suez Canal was a defining moment in Arab nationalism.

Nasser introduced socialist reforms throughout Egypt—nationalizing land and banks—although the effect was at times more symbolic than economically beneficial. He did, however, break decisively with Egypt's near-feudal past, and attempted to modernize and industrialize the country, raising educational standards and significantly enhancing the role of women. Charming and personable as an individual, as a politician Nasser kept all opposition at bay by running a repressive police state.

He achieved unprecedented popularity throughout the Arab world and became one of the founding leaders of the Non-Aligned Movement of countries that were supposedly free from either East or West, even though in the final analysis he was closely allied to the Soviet Union. Fiercely anti-Israel, he attempted to unite the Arab world, setting up a federation of Egypt and Syria and forming the United Arab Republic under his presidency. But the union

broke down in 1961, following a military coup in Syria.

Nasser led Egypt into a disastrous war against Israel in 1967, when his army was completely routed. He never fully recovered from the blow. He resigned but was persuaded to stay on. Three years later, after struggling to rebuild the army and national morale, he died from a heart attack.

Chronology

1918	Born in Alexandria, January 15
1936	Enters military college
1938	Graduates as officer in Egyptian army
1948	First Arab–Israeli war
1952	Bloodless coup overthrows King Farouk
1954	Nasser assumes power
1956	Egypt nationalizes Suez Canal
1967	Egypt defeated by Israel in Six Day War
1970	Dies in Cairo after heart attack, September 28

Ronald Reagan

Ronald Reagan (1911–2004), a former movie star who became the 40th President of the United States, was known as the "great communicator." A Republican, he reestablished conservative politics at home and won the Cold War.

Born in Tampico, Illinois, the son of an Irish-American alcoholic shoe salesman, Reagan attended high school in nearby Dixon, and worked his way through Eureka College, where he earned a degree in economics and sociology, played football, and acted. After college he became a radio sports announcer, and took a screen test in 1937 to win a contract at Warner Brothers in Hollywood. During the next two decades he acted in a total of fifty-three films, mostly B movies. He also appeared in training films for the army during World War II. His wartime marriage to actress Jane Wyman failed, and he married another actress, Nancy Davis, in 1952.

"Surround yourself with the best people you can, delegate authority, and don't interfere"

Reagan became involved in politics as president of the Screen Actors Guild, which was then embroiled in the issue of Communism in the film industry. He shifted from liberal to conservative, and toured the country as a television host and public relations speaker, becoming an increasingly popular spokesman for the Republican right. In 1966, he was elected governor of California by a margin of a million votes, and he was reelected in 1970. He established his own style as governor, delegating most of the day-to-day business and concentrating only on the larger policy issues. He also learned how to exploit television to marshal popular support.

Ten years later, and following two failed bids for the nomination, Reagan swept into the White House on a conservative platform, winning 51 percent of the vote to beat Jimmy Carter, mainly due to Carter's poor management of the economy and bungling of the crisis over the

Chronology

1911	Born in Tampico, Illinois, February 6
1932	Graduates from Eureka College, first job on radio
1937	First Hollywood film contract
1966	Elected governor of California
1970	Reelected governor
1980	Wins presidential election, beating Jimmy Carter
1981	Takes office as 40th President of the United States
1984	Wins second term as U.S. President
1989	Leaves office
1994	Withdraws from public life with Alzheimer's
2004	Dies aged 95

American hostages in Iran. Reagan and his vice-president George Bush trounced the Democrats again in 1984, winning 59 percent of the vote to earn a second term.

On the domestic front, Reagan stuck to his election promises; he cut taxes and government spending, and persuaded Congress to vote in measures to stimulate the economy. His opponents lambasted his economic policy as "Reaganomics;" unemployment initially soared, as did the budget deficit, but in the end his policies delivered a decade of growth. He was tough with unions—in a typical move he had the nation's air traffic controllers sacked for striking.

Abroad, Reagan sought to achieve "peace through strength," and he upped the ante in the Cold War by increasing defense spending by 35 percent over his eight years in office, and by launching his "Star Wars" program to create a defense shield in space. He struck up a special relationship with British Prime Minister Margaret Thatcher, and working in close harmony they in turn threatened and wooed the Soviet Union, which Reagan had denounced early in his presidency as "an evil empire." Reagan's summits with Soviet President Mikhail Gorbachev led to a major nuclear arms treaty in 1987 and ultimately fostered the climate that resulted in the peaceful dismantling of the Soviet Empire. Reagan also took his war on Communism to Nicaragua in Central America and he tackled the perceived source of international terrorism by bombing Libya.

As in some of his cowboy film roles, Reagan kept things simple. He had clarity of vision—whether on government spending or getting rid of Communism—and he was able to communicate his message well and consistently.

Reagan survived an assassination attempt on his sixty-ninth day in office, an event that gave the actor his first major role on the world stage. He said he had forgotten to duck, a joke in keeping with his affable, folksy charm. "I hope you're all Republicans," he said as he was wheeled into the operating room. Reagan's broadcasts to the nation at times of crisis, and on occasions such as the Challenger Shuttle disaster in 1986, were brilliant performances that seemed to come straight from the heart. They more than justified his reputation as the "great communicator" and perhaps enabled him also to become the "great escaper" when, for example, he managed to dodge responsibility for the arms-for-hostages Iran-Contra Affair.

Reagan retired to his Los Angeles home and wrote his autobiography, *An American Life* (1990). A poignant letter to the American people in 1994 announced his withdrawal from public life because he was suffering from Alzheimer's disease. Reagan died in 2004, aged 93.

Memorable Quotes

■ "Mr Gorbachev, open this gate. Mr Gorbachev, tear down this wall!"

■ "There are no such things as limits to growth, because there are no limits on the human capacity for intelligence, imagination, and wonder."

■ "Surround yourself with the best people you can find, delegate authority, and don't interfere."

■ "Welfare's purpose should be to eliminate, as far as possible, the need for its own existence."

■ "It is the Soviet Union that runs against the tide of history... (It is) the march of freedom and democracy which will leave Marxism-Leninism on the ash heap of history."

Margaret Thatcher

Baroness Margaret Thatcher of Kesteven (1925–) was British Prime Minister for an unbroken eleven years, during which she won a war in the South Atlantic, helped bring down Soviet Communism, and reasserted the triumph of capitalism at home and abroad. She was Britain's first woman prime minister.

Born Hilda Margaret Roberts, Thatcher was the daughter of a shopkeeper from Grantham, England. She took a degree in chemistry at Oxford University and became a barrister specializing in tax law, married a wealthy businessman, Denis Thatcher, and was elected to Parliament for the London constituency of Finchley in 1959.

Thatcher first entered the Cabinet as Education Secretary in 1970 in the government of Edward Heath, and she challenged Heath for the party leadership after he lost two general elections in 1975. To the surprise of many, and the lasting bitterness of the centrist Heath, the crusading anti-socialist Thatcher won.

She swept to power in the general election in 1979 and had an uneasy start: her policy of rolling back the frontiers of the state, freeing up business and industry from government interference and subsidies, while clamping down on public expenditure, produced spiraling interest rates and high unemployment. The number out of work peaked at three million. But she stuck defiantly to her belief that market forces alone would create lasting prosperity.

She bolstered her reputation by leading the country in a war against Argentina to recover the Falkland Islands, a remote British dependency in the South Atlantic, which Argentina had invaded in pursuit of long-standing territorial claims. The war was highly risky; but it showed the world and Britain that Thatcher had steel. Soon after recovering the Falklands, Thatcher won a landslide election victory over a weak and divided opposition for a second term.

Her second government pursued a more radical program of privatization and deregulation, reform of the trade unions to curtail their power once and for all, tax cuts, and introduction of free market mechanisms into health and education. In 1984–5 she won a major confrontation with striking coal miners, who staged nationwide protests in their bid to keep the pits open with state subsidies. The sale of state-owned enterprises continued

"The lady's not for turning"

apace until virtually nothing but health, education, and defense was left on the state payroll—telecommunications, aerospace, television, radio, gas, electricity, water, the state airline, British steel, and public housing were all sold off. The number of individual shareholders in Britain tripled, while one and a half million people purchased their state-owned homes. Her

The Wisdom of Thatcher

Some legendary quotes:

■ "Economics are the method; the object is to change the soul."

■ "It will be years before a woman either leads the Conservative Party or becomes prime minister. I don't see it happening in my time."

■ "I am extraordinarily patient, provided I get my own way in the end."

■ Margaret Thatcher was the longest consecutively serving prime minister for more than 150 years (since Lord Liverpool). Her total time as prime minister was 11 years, 209 days.

■ Her hardline, uncompromising approach and combative style of government acquired its own name—Thatcherism.

■ "You turn if you want to. The lady's not for turning."

policy of privatization caught on around the world, and by the end of the decade more than fifty countries had started similar programs.

A bomb planted by the Irish Republican Army (IRA) almost killed Thatcher at a Conservative Party conference in Brighton in 1984—attempted revenge for her refusal to negotiate with Republican hunger strikers, ten of whom starved themselves to death in British jails in Northern Ireland.

Thatcher demonstrated her steely will again in 1986 when she abolished London's governing body, the Greater London Council; she had no time for its socialist leader Ken Livingstone.

Thatcher won a record third term in 1987. She had by now become a world leader and had struck up an especially close relationship with U.S. President Ronald Reagan, which had paid dividends in American support during the Falklands conflict. Both leaders openly set out to bring down what they saw as the "evil empire" of Soviet Communism, earning Thatcher a backhanded compliment from Soviet leader Mikhail Gorbachev, who dubbed her the "Iron Lady." Thatcher vigorously supported Reagan's policy of rearming, which brought the Soviets to the negotiating table, set off perestroika and eventually led to the collapse of Communism.

In 1989, Thatcher introduced a widely unpopular community "poll tax," sparking angry riots. Meanwhile, her heavy-handed dealings with her own Cabinet and her increasingly strident opposition to the European Union led to several stormy resignations—notably her Defence Secretary Michael Heseltine and, in 1990, her long-serving Foreign Secretary Geoffrey Howe. His resignation speech in Parliament set in train the events that led to Thatcher's downfall a few weeks later. Heseltine challenged her for the leadership and, while he failed to win, he gained enough votes to persuade her that a crucial minority of the party favored change. She resigned, and two years later Thatcher quit front-line politics and took a seat in the upper House of Lords as Baroness.

Chronology

1925	Born in Grantham, Lincolnshire, England, October 13
1959	Entered Parliament
1975	Tory leader
1979	Prime Minister
1982	Falklands War
1983	Wins second general election
1987	Wins third general election
1990	Loses party leadership

Mikhail Gorbachev

Mikhail Gorbachev (1931–) was the last Soviet leader. He ushered out Communist rule in Russia and East Europe and helped end the Cold War. Hailed in the West as a great liberator, he was reviled by many in his own homeland for the collapse of the Soviet Empire.

There was little in his early career to suggest that Mikhail Sergeyevich Gorbachev would become the leader to dismantle the Soviet Empire. He was born into a peasant family near Stavropol in southwestern Russia in 1931; he joined the Communist Party and drove a combine harvester at a state farm for four years before leaving for Moscow, where he took a degree in law at the State University. He worked his way up the party apparatus in his home region of Stavropol and, under the wing of two senior Politburo members, Mikhail Suslov and Yuri Andropov, he was elected on to the Communist Party's Central Committee in 1971. In 1978 he was put in charge of Soviet agriculture. He already knew about the inefficiencies of the collective system from his own family background, but he now had to grapple with it.

In 1980 Gorbachev became a full member of the Politburo, the Soviet Union's highest policy-making body, and two years later his mentor, Andropov, succeeded Leonid Brezhnev as Soviet leader. Andropov continued to push Gorbachev, who was now building a reputation as an enemy of corruption and inefficiency. Brimming with self-confidence, Gorbachev took over as Soviet party leader in March 1985, and became President of the USSR in 1988.

Mikhail Gorbachev changed the world, but lost his own country while doing so

From the outset, he was a man in a hurry. He strove to reform the highly inefficient and now stagnant state-run economy: glasnost (openness) and perestroika (restructuring) became the keynotes of his six-year rule. Realizing that the Soviet economy was virtually bankrupt and that

Chronology

1931	Born in Privolnoye near Stavropol, March 2
1955	Graduates in law from Moscow University
1971	Elected to Central Committee
1978	Party Secretary in charge of agriculture
1980	Joins Politburo
1985	General Secretary of Soviet Communist Party
1987	Agreement with United States to scrap intermediate-range nuclear-tipped missiles
1988	President of the USSR
1990	Fall of the Berlin Wall
1990	Awarded Nobel Peace Prize
1991	Survives attempted coup against him
1991	Gorbachev resigns as President of defunct USSR

the capitalist West had far outstripped it in terms of new technology, Gorbachev also began to argue for an end to the costly arms race with the West.

It is always said that the most dangerous moment for a dictatorship is when it begins to liberalize, and Gorbachev soon found himself caught between the party establishment, who saw its privileges threatened by a free press, elections, and market economy reforms, and the radicals who wanted to do away at once with the one-party state and the command economy. Gorbachev introduced a new partially elected parliament, the Congress of People's Deputies, and, in 1989, was duly elected its chairman. But he never quite dared go all the way in freeing the economy from state control, and in the resulting chaos and confusion he all but lost

control at home. He had also unleashed forces of nationalism in the Baltics and other Soviet republics, which were to prove unstoppable. The success he achieved in negotiating new arms control agreements with the United States and in withdrawing Soviet troops from Afghanistan led to the peaceful breakaway of former Communist countries in Asia and eastern Europe, and to the reunification of Germany—all welcomed in the West as the start of a new era. At home, and to hardline Communists, it all appeared a sell-out.

Hardliners and their military supporters struck back in August 1991 and staged a coup while Gorbachev was on vacation in the Crimea. The coup collapsed, in large part because of the courage of Moscow street demonstrators and of the President of Russia, Boris Yeltsin. Gorbachev was restored to office, but power now belonged to the leaders of the various republics, above all to Yeltsin. On December 25, 1991, Gorbachev resigned and the Soviet Union ceased to exist. In 2007 he returned to politics, becoming leader of the Union of Social Democrats.

An "Accidental" Hero

■ Did Gorbachev plan the break-up of the Soviet Union? Almost certainly not from the start. Gorbachev zigzagged through history, but his lasting achievement was that his—probably unintended—dismantling of one of the most heavily armed empires in history was achieved without major bloodshed.

■ Gorbachev remained active in politics but got nowhere in the new Russia of Boris Yeltsin. He stood in the 1996 presidential elections, but failed to attract much support. He was a hit on the American and European lecture circuit, and even used his popularity to sell a pizza brand in a U.S. television spot.

■ Gorbachev was the first Soviet leader to "market" his wife. The strikingly attractive Raisa would accompany him on visits, bringing him admirers in the West, but the Russians, unaccustomed to "First Ladies," resented her. Raisa died of leukaemia in 1999, and Gorbachev won great sympathy for his display of grief at her death.

Alexander the Great

Alexander the Great (356–323 BCE), King of Macedonia, was one of the great military leaders: he conquered half the known world in thirteen years, and never lost a battle. His achievement was to spread Hellenic culture from Gibraltar on the Atlantic seaboard to the Punjab in India.

Alexander became King of Macedonia in 336 BCE after his father, King Philip II, was assassinated. Not yet twenty, he inherited a prosperous kingdom with a professional standing army that dominated Greece's city-states. Alexander, who had been raised in the art of warfare by his father and tutored by Aristotle, swiftly consolidated his hold on Greece, with a combination of force and diplomacy, and was elected supreme commander of the Greek forces for a war against Asia. He spent the next year putting down regional rebellions and crushing a revolt in Thebes.

Alexander led one of the world's greatest military machines. Well-trained infantry, deployed in phalanx formations and supported by cavalry, provided the cutting edge and backbone of the Macedonian army; Alexander's success often derived from the careful coordination of light horse and foot soldiers by which he would surprise and outmaneuver far larger forces. Alexander was also a master of the siege. Above all, he led his men from the front. He was wounded in battle at least seven times, most seriously when an arrow pierced his lung in India.

He crossed the Dardanelles in 334 BCE, and went straight to Troy—now in modern Turkey and the site of the great victory of the Greeks over Asia—and it was near here that he won a major victory against the Persians at Granicus River. The following year Alexander

overwhelmed a far bigger force of Persians, led by their king, Darius, at Issus in what is now northeastern Syria. Alexander now knew he could take Persia, but first he secured the eastern Mediterranean—invading Syria and then capturing Tyre after a seven-month siege, brilliantly executed by building a causeway to the island fortress.

Alexander was a master of all kinds of warfare, but above all he led his men from the front

Gaza and Egypt fell and, after a suitable spell among his new Egyptian subjects and a pilgrimage to their shrine of Amon-Ra in the Libyan desert, Alexander reassembled his forces in Tyre and set out for Babylon. Crossing the Tigris and Euphrates, he met King Darius on the plains of modern-day northern Iraq and inflicted a crushing defeat on him at Gaugamela in 331 BCE. Darius fled but was later slain. Over the next three years, Alexander subdued Persia and set about creating an eastern empire, appointing local officials and even going native, adopting Persian dress and marrying a Persian, Roxana.

Alexander now spent two years fighting in what is modern-day Afghanistan, pressing as far north as the Oxus River, before announcing his intention of conquering India. He crossed the Indus River in 326 BCE and invaded the Punjab as far as the river Hyphasis. By now he had realized that the subcontinent was bigger than he had been led to believe; his fellow Macedonians refused to go on, and their iron-willed leader

Cutting the Gordian Knot

■ The Gordian knot was fiendishly difficult and had no open ends. Legend had it that he who loosed it would conquer Asia. With characteristic decisiveness, Alexander was said to have taken one look and sliced it through with a sword. "What difference does it make how I loose it?" he asked. To cut the Gordian knot has come to mean slicing through a problem that appears hopelessly complex by some simple, bold stroke.

■ Alexander is said to have tamed the wild black stallion Bucephalus when he was aged only ten. Bucephalus was his favorite mount and he named a city in India after the horse when it died with him on his 327 BCE campaign throughout that country.

■ Alexander and his successors founded some seventy cities, most famous among them Alexandria, at the mouth of the Nile, in Egypt, in 332 BCE.

halted the push into India. Alexander notched up one more victory, defeating a force led by King Porus in 326 BCE after his men had overcome their terror of facing elephants in battle, and his army then returned home by land and sea.

Back in Persia, Alexander set about organizing his empire. He imposed a bizarre mix of potentate central control—executing bad governors and introducing a single currency—with the fostering of a looser federation based on coexistence and racial equality, something his fellow Macedonians did not like at all. He was in the end full of contradictions—driven and yet flexible, a dreamer and a strategist, cruel and kind, and given to murderous fits of rage, often directed at those closest to him. Immensely good looking, he seems at times to have believed in his own divine origins. He was preparing an invasion of Arabia when he died of fever in Babylon in 323 BCE, most probably after another of his notorious drinking bouts, although some sources suggest he was poisoned.

Chronology

356 BCE	Born in Pella, ancient capital of Macedonia
336 BCE	King of Macedonia
334 BCE	Leads Greek invasion of Persia
334 BCE	Battle of Granicus
333 BCE	Battle of Issus
331 BCE	Battle of Gaugamela
327 BCE	Enters India
324 BCE	Returns to Persia
323 BCE	Dies in Babylon on June 13

Hannibal

Hannibal, a Carthaginian general (247–183 BCE), spent almost his entire adult life fighting Rome, most of it with unparalleled success. His great achievement was to invade Italy through the back door—over the Alps.

Hannibal was the son of Hamilcar Barca, the general who commanded the Carthaginian forces in Sicily during the first of the three great Punic Wars, a struggle for mastery of the Mediterranean between an aggressively expansionist Rome and the seafaring state of Carthage. After he was defeated by the Romans and driven from Sicily, Hamilcar set about repositioning Carthage by building up its power in Spain.

Aged only nine, Hannibal accompanied his father to Spain, and before he left he swore a solemn oath of enmity to Rome. He was to remain true to that vow all his life.

Hannibal grew up to fight successful campaigns in Spain, and in 221 BCE, on the death of his brother-in-law Hasdrubal and aged only twenty-six, he was appointed commander in chief of the Carthaginian forces. He was a brilliant tactician, using intelligence to the utmost, sending scouts into enemy camps and even at times going behind enemy lines himself. He always seemed to be able to second-guess the enemy; he became the master of the pincer movement. Within two years he had consolidated Carthage's hold on the Iberian Peninsula, with the exception of the Roman outpost of Sanguntum, which he overran after an eight-month siege. This sparked a new war between Rome and Carthage—the Second Punic War (218–201 BCE).

The Punic Wars

■ The Punic Wars derive their name from Punica, the Latin for Phoenicia, from where the Carthaginians originally came. Rome won all three wars.

■ Livy's *History of Rome* highlights Hannibal's military successes as he swept through Italy after crossing the Alps. He called the battle at Lake Trasimeno "one of the few memorable disasters to Roman arms."

■ Although Livy painted Hannibal as a cruel and uncouth soldier, he was in fact a cultured Greek scholar who could compose state papers in Greek and who also wrote books.

Hannibal's daring would now win him an unsurpassed place in military history; he undertook one of the great outflanking movements of all times. Italy was too heavily defended by sea, so Hannibal decided to go the long way round. Hannibal's march on Rome began in 218 BCE. He set out from New Carthage (now the Spanish city of Cartagena), at the head of a force of 40,000, including cavalry and elephants, and stormed over the Pyrenees through southern France, and then, in just fifteen days, he crossed the Alps, by either the Col de Grimone or the Col de Cabre. This was an extraordinary feat for an army used to operating in hot plains. How many men were lost to the hostile terrain, cold, and guerrilla attacks remains a matter of conjecture, but Hannibal emerged on the other side with at least one elephant and a fighting force of foot soldiers and cavalry. His invasion of northern Italy was the equivalent of the United States' Pearl Harbor: Rome was stunned. Hannibal pushed on

Far from the cruel, uncouth soldier he is sometimes portrayed as, Hannibal was a cultured Greek scholar

south, cutting down whole armies of Romans in a string of punishing victories, culminating at Lake Trasimeno, where contemporary accounts say the water was turned red with the blood of Gaius Flaminius's army. Rome was probably, at that stage, his for the taking, but he hesitated.

Hannibal's campaign in Italy continued for fifteen more years and, although he inflicted another crushing defeat on a Roman army in 216 BCE at Cannae on the Aufidus (Ofanto) River, he never quite got the upper hand again—in part because of a change in Roman tactics. Rather than confront him in open battle, they harried him and ground him down. Also, reinforcements failed to arrive. Hannibal was progressively pushed back to the south.

In 204 BCE, his nemesis Scipio seized the initiative and landed in North Africa; Hannibal was ordered to return to Carthage. The two generals clashed at Zama in 202 BCE, and Hannibal, let down by Numidian horsemen who changed sides, was finally defeated by Scipio. Carthage capitulated to Rome, and the Second Punic War ended, and Scipio returned in triumph bearing the title "Africanus."

Hannibal successfully set about restoring Carthage's fortunes, proving to be an effective peacetime leader, but, under pressure from Rome, he was driven into exile. He went on to fight the Romans from Syria, but when Syria fell into Roman hands in 190 BCE, Hannibal moved further east. He was finally trapped in Bythnia, in northern Asia Minor, where he committed suicide by drinking poison from the casket on the ring he always wore—probably in the year 183 BCE.

Chronology

247 BCE	Born in Carthage
221 BCE	Hannibal appointed commander in chief
218 BCE	Start of Second Punic War
218 BCE	Hannibal invades Italy
217 BCE	Defeats Gaius Flaminias at Lake Trasimeno
216 BCE	Inflicts worst defeat on Roman army at Cannae
203 BCE	Hannibal recalled to Carthage
202 BCE	Hannibal defeated by Scipio Africanus at Zama
183 BCE	Dies by taking poison

Julius Caesar

Gaius Julius Caesar (100–44 BCE), Roman general and statesman, extended Rome's rule into western Europe and laid the foundations of the Roman Empire. A superb and daring general, who inspired loyalty in his soldiers, he was also an enlightened administrator, a writer, and a famous lover. His detractors saw him as a tyrant, who saw himself as a god and allowed Rome's republican system of government to collapse.

Julius Caesar was born into the prestigious Julian clan and was always destined for high office. As a young man he acquired his first taste of power thanks to his aunt's husband, the great general Gaius Marius, who appointed him to the position of priest of Jupiter, the chief god of the Roman people. But Marius died soon after, and Caesar left Rome and traveled east to fight with the legions and gain his first experience of warfare. He later returned to Rome to study and practice law and then spent time in Rhodes learning oratory. On the way there he was kidnapped by and escaped from pirates, whom he later captured and crucified. Returning to Rome, he started working his way up the political ladder. Elected quaestor in 68 BCE, he served time in southern Spain and, with a lavish lifestyle and new wife to support, began to enjoy the patronage of Rome's richest man, Marcus Licinius Crassus. By 60 BCE Caesar was established with Crassus and Pompey as one of the three masters of Rome in what was known as the First Triumvirate. But instead of a military command, Caesar was assigned to the care of the roads and forests.

This unglamorous appointment was a turning point. With trouble brewing on the Rhine, Caesar lobbied hard to be given military command of the territories north of the Alps. Rome had hitherto concentrated most of her might on consolidating in the Mediterranean. The decision to send Caesar north would transform what was to become the Roman Empire and lay the foundations of modern Europe.

This was his brilliant period—the seven years of the Gallic Wars in which Caesar notched up a string of victories over the Helveti, Germans, Nervi, and Belgae, as he gradually consolidated Rome's rule over central and northern Europe west of the Rhine. The achievement was all the more remarkable because the north European barbarians were on the whole an even match for the Romans. Caesar prevailed through his mastery of strategy and tactics and the discipline of his soldiers. He was at the same time a ruler of vision, respecting local customs and giving a system of government and rights of citizenship to the conquered. There were setbacks and defeats, too; two expeditions to England, in 55 BCE and 54 BCE, came to nothing, and the Gallic leader, Vercingetorix, forced his army off the field at Gergovia, near modern Clermont-

Veni, Vidi, Vici

■ Caesar was the author of several great works (most of them lost), including self-serving but brilliant accounts of his Gallic Wars and the civil war against Pompey.

Memorable statements:

■ "Veni, Vidi, Vici" (I came, I saw, I conquered), about his successful campaign against Mithridate's son, Pharnaces (a supporter of Pompey), in 47 BCE.

■ "Et Tu, Brute" (You, too, Brutus), his last words, on realizing that even his closest companion, Marcus Junius Brutus, had betrayed him. They may, however, have been spoken in Greek.

■ The word Caesar lived on as Kaiser and Tsar.

Caesar notched up a string of victories as he consolidated Roman rule over Europe

he was emperor of a republic. Ultimately it was this contradiction, combined with his magnanimity and vanity, that turned his friends against him; he was cut down in the Senate with twenty-three stab wounds on the Ides of March. The people had loved Caesar, and Romans rose in anger against the conspirators; the chaos that followed ultimately resulted in Caesar's great-nephew Octavius taking power. He, as Augustus, established the Roman Empire.

Caesar introduced the Julian calendar; the month of July is named after him. It began on January 1, 45 BCE.

Ferrand, in 52 BCE. But Caesar's star was in the ascendant and when in 52 BCE Pompey seized control and ordered Caesar's army to disband, the battle-hardened and power-hungry general disobeyed, and marched on Rome. "The die is cast," he said, as he crossed the Rubicon, a small stream separating his province of Cisalpine Gaul from Italy.

The move sparked civil war, which lasted on and off for four years, even though Caesar swiftly overwhelmed Rome and proceeded to crush Pompey at the battle of Pharsalus, in Greece. Caesar then moved on to Egypt, where he fell into the amorous arms of Cleopatra. More campaigns followed—in Asia Minor, North Africa, and Spain—and when he returned to Rome for the final time in 45 BCE he had been at war more or less without a break for thirteen years. Back in Rome, he became dictator for life, thus quashing the power of the now discredited Roman nobility. He used the title Imperator; in effect

Chronology

100 BCE	Born in Rome on July 12 or 13
60 BCE	Member of the First Triumvirate
59 BCE	Elected Consul
58 BCE	Governor of Gaul
55 BCE	First expedition to Britain
49 BCE	Returns to Rome, crossing the Rubicon
48 BCE	Defeats Pompey at battle of Pharsalus
44 BCE	Murdered on steps of Senate on March 15

William the Conqueror

William the Conqueror (1027–87), Duke of Normandy and King of England, led the last successful invasion of the British Isles. One of the great soldiers and rulers of the Middle Ages, William established England's Anglo-Norman dynasty, subdued the turbulent Welsh and Scottish borders, and left a monumental testament to royal administrative power and public record keeping, the Domesday Book.

William "the Bastard" was appointed Duke of Normandy at the age of eight, the illegitimate son of Duke Robert I and Arlette, a tanner's daughter. With many of his father's family all too eager to profit from his death, and the legitimacy of his position tenuous as a bastard heir, his childhood was beset with danger: three of his guardians died violently and his tutor was murdered. William's successful personal rule of the duchy began in 1042, consolidating the power of the ducal family over rebellious barons and asserting his independence from the French king, whose authority as royal overlord of Normandy was reduced to that of a nominal figurehead for the following 150 years.

Having successfully subdued his own territory, the duke set his sights on greater riches

William's claim to the English throne started taking shape from 1052, when he opened negotiations with his cousin Edward the Confessor to build an alliance in the face of rebellions on his eastern borders. Norman chroniclers, writing after the Conquest, went as far as to allege, improbably, that the heirless King of England had even promised the Norman duke the English throne, supposedly then confirmed by Harold, Earl of Wessex, during a trip to Normandy around 1064.

However, when Edward died childless in January 1066, Harold was himself crowned king, much to William's fury. Having successfully subdued his duchy, the duke had now set his sights on greater territorial riches: the wealth of the nearby isles presented an irresistible challenge. William's soldiers crossed the Channel in September of that year, met just in time by King Harold, who had rushed back to the south coast after fighting off another rival claimant to the throne, Harald Hardraada. After a 250-mile (400 km) march from Stamford Bridge, near York, the English troops put up a strong fight at Hastings but were outdone by the Normans' fresh troops and cavalry, and outwitted by their cunning tactic of feigned retreat. Harold was killed toward dusk on October 14 1066, and William was crowned King of England at Westminster Abbey on Christmas Day. To show he was now in control, William ordered the construction of the Tower of London as his fortress.

William I was a king of his time, a man of iron will, who applied brutal methods of government to maintain peace and administer justice. The first three years of his reign were spent crushing localized rebellions, notably in the west and north, and in securing the historically turbulent Welsh and Scottish borders. He created the defensive marcher counties along these after his successful invasions of Scotland in 1072 and Wales in 1081. With the conquest complete,

Chronology

1027	Born in Falaise, Normandy
1035	Duke of Normandy, "William the Bastard"
1066	Defeats King Harold at Hastings and crowned King of England
1086	Orders the Domesday survey
1087	Dies at Rouen, September 9

William selected loyal experts to run his new kingdom during his prolonged absences in Normandy; much of the successes of Anglo-Norman government can be attributed to his old friend Lanfranc, whom he made Archbishop of Canterbury.

In 1086, William ordered a full survey to be made of his kingdom, resulting in the compilation of the Domesday Book, a tribute to the sophisticated machinery of Anglo-Saxon local government and Norman efficiency in utilizing it. Abroad, William was threatened by an alliance of Philip I of France and his own son, Robert Curthose. This angered the king so much that on his deathbed in 1087, having been mortally wounded by the pommel of his horse's saddle in Mantes, he deprived Robert of his English inheritance and gave it instead to his second born, William Rufus, while Robert was left with Normandy.

Unprecedented Power

■ Contemporaries regarded William as a more powerful king than any of his Anglo-Saxon predecessors; they were overawed by the almost merciless imposition of his royal power, and by his success in wiping out virtually all trace of the old English ruling class. Indeed, Williams's revolution was so complete that within twenty years, the entire ruling class of church and state spoke French. Church chroniclers glossed over what was an essentially violent life, portraying William with a veneer of legitimacy and respectability; however, the inscription on his tombstone at Caen presents a perhaps more accurate summary of the life of this warrior king:

He ruled the savage Normans; Britain's men
He courageously conquered, and kept them in
*   his power*
And bravely thrust back swords from Maine
And made them subject to his rule's laws
William the great king lies in this little urn,
So small a house serves for a mighty lord.

Saladin

Saladin (1138–93), Sultan of Egypt and Syria, reunited the Arabs and led a "jihad," a holy war, against the Christian Crusaders, recapturing Jerusalem for the Muslims and successfully fending off the great counter-offensive of the Third Crusade.

Salah al-din Yusuf ibn Ayyub, or Saladin as he is popularly known, was born in 1138 in Tikrit, now in Iraq, and was of Kurdish descent. It was a time of disunity among Arabs, with much of Palestine, including Jerusalem, in the hands of foreigners from Western Europe—the Christian Crusaders. Saladin learned to fight them from an early age. He was only fourteen when he entered into the service of his uncle, the Syrian military commander Asad ad-Din Shirkuh, with whom he fought with distinction on three expeditions

to help the decadent Fatimid caliphate of Egypt against the Crusaders. On his uncle's death, in 1169, Saladin became commander in chief of the Syrian army and vizier of Egypt. He quickly established a power base in Cairo, and in 1171 he toppled the weak and unpopular Shi'ite Fatimid regime and brought Egypt back under the Abbasid caliphate and Sunni law; in the process he founded the Ayyubib dynasty.

He had to use his wits to survive the ensuing complex power struggles of the divided Holy

Land, and he could well have met an inglorious end had it not been for the timely deaths in 1174 of the Syrian Emir Nur ed-Din, and of Amalric, the King of Christian Jerusalem. The way was now open for Saladin to take control of Syria, and from then on he worked tirelessly to bring the feuding Muslim territories of the Middle East under one banner with the single purpose of driving out the Crusaders. He consolidated his hold over Muslim lands from Egypt to the borders of Persia, engaging in an on-off frontier war with the Crusaders until finally, on June 30, 1187, he crossed the Jordan and launched an all-out invasion of the now weakened and internally riven Latin Kingdom.

The end came with unexpected swiftness. Saladin lured the Christians into a waterless trap on the Horns of Hattin, a rocky escarpment above the Sea of Galilee near Tiberias, and, on a scorching summer day, July 4, 1187, he inflicted a crushing defeat on their thirst-wracked army. Saladin was magnanimous to the defeated King Guy and to his lay barons, but he had the surviving Templar and Hospitaller knights beheaded, and the remaining soldiers sold into slavery. The price of a captive Christian in Damascus dropped to three dinars, and one prisoner was bartered for a pair of sandals.

A military genius, he was honored alike by his enemies and his own people for his chivalry

The mighty Crusader castles now fell to Saladin one by one—with the exception of Tyre—and less than three months later, on October 2, he had taken Jerusalem, but in stark

A Chivalrous Warrior

■ Saladin was no great beauty—he was short and stout, red-faced, and blind in one eye—but he exercised a fascination over his Christian contemporaries and remains a captivating figure even today. His chivalry challenged the Crusaders as much as his courage on the battlefield. There is even a suggestion by some sources that Saladin was secretly knighted by Humphrey of Toron; perhaps this was the Crusaders' way of explaining his chivalry. Although Saladin could be harsh, and he never hesitated to use the sword and even crucified some Shi'a opponents, there are countless accounts of his acts of chivalry toward the Crusaders; he once sent fresh fruit to the sick King Richard and snow from Mount Hermon to cool his drinks.

■ Jerusalem, a holy city to the world's three great monotheistic religions, Judaism, Christianity, and Islam, has been fought over for centuries. It remains a contested city to this day.

Chronology

1138	Born in Tikrit, modern Iraq
1169	Commander of Syrian army; Vizier of Egypt
1171	Seizes power in Egypt
1174	Seizes power in Syria; unites Muslims
1187	Battle of Horns of Hattin. Recaptures Jerusalem
1193	Dies in Damascus on March 4

contrast to the way the Crusaders had entered the city eighty-eight years before, this time there was no looting and no bloodshed.

The fall of Jerusalem provoked an angry response in Western Europe and no fewer than three monarchs set out at the head of a massive counter-attack—the Third Crusade. Led by the King of England, Richard I, the Crusaders took back Acre in 1191, but failed in their primary objective—Jerusalem. Richard got the better of Saladin at the battle of Arsuf later the same year, but it was little more than an indecisive skirmish; the war itself was a stalemate. In 1192 Saladin concluded an armistice agreement with Richard, which left the Crusaders in command of the coastal cities, and the bulk of Palestine, including Jerusalem, in the hands of the Muslims.

Saladin died the following year in Damascus, on March 4, ill and worn out by years of warfare.

St. Joan of Arc

Joan of Arc (1412–31) was an illiterate peasant girl, inspired by visions to expel the English from France during the Hundred Years' War. She did not succeed. Captured, tried, and burnt at the stake, her bravery nonetheless rallied the French and their king at a critical moment.

Joan of Arc was born to a peasant farming family in the village of Domrémy near the borders of the province of Lorraine. As a young girl she claimed regularly to hear voices, which she later identified as St. Michael, St. Catherine, and St. Margaret. In May 1428 her voices urged her to go to the King of France and help him reconquer his kingdom from the English. At this time French king Charles VII was still uncrowned, and known as the Dauphin. The English king, Henry VI, claimed the French crown and was supported by the Duke of Burgundy, the Dauphin's uncle, in campaigns to occupy large areas of northern France.

Joan went to the nearest French enclave in Vaucouleurs and demanded to see the king. She was only sixteen, and she and her visions were not taken seriously. The following year, 1429, dressed in men's clothes, she made her way to Chinon, where she immediately recognized the Dauphin, who had hidden among his courtiers. Charles was at first sceptical of Joan urging battle against the English, but changed his mind after she had been intensively examined by theologians. Her rallying cry gave new energy to the French. She was given a small military force, and adopted a suit of white armor, and a banner with the fleur-de-lys. Joan—who was only seventeen—gave new energy to the French and inspired them to a decisive victory over the English in May 1429 at the relief of Orléans. This led to parts of northern France, which had previously sided with the English, declaring their loyalty to Charles.

Her insistence on her "voices" from God was seen as heretical defiance: Joan was burnt at the stake

Called by God

■ When Joan was burnt at the stake she asked a Dominican monk to hold up a crucifix, and shout out words of salvation so she could hear them above the crackle of the flames. After she died her body was shown to the crowds, before it was completely incinerated. Her ashes were scattered in the Seine River, near Rouen.

■ Her youth, pious convictions, common sense, and heroism have inspired plays, poems, films, and biographies by German, French, English, and American writers, including Schiller, Shaw, Anouilh, Voltaire, and Twain.

■ When not in a suit of white armor, Joan dressed in knightly attire of cloth of gold and silk trimmed with fur and a doublet and hose.

The Dauphin was crowned King Charles VII at Rheims on July 17, 1429, with Joan standing near him holding her banner. This was a daring move as Rheims, the traditional coronation site for French kings, was in enemy territory.

Charles was indecisive about attacking Paris, then in Burgundian hands, but Joan felt it was essential to take the city; she became impatient, and on September 8 1429 she was waving her banner on the fortifications and urging the Parisians to surrender to the French troops. Wounded, she was hailed as a heroine who had put an end to English supremacy in France. She and her family were ennobled by the king.

But Charles vacillated and opposed all further plans to fight against the English and their Burgundian allies. Joan, independently, in May 1430, led a campaign against the enemy at Compiègne. She was unhorsed and taken prisoner by the Burgundians who handed her over to the English representative, Pierre Cauchon, Bishop of Beauvais, in exchange for 10,000 francs. For fourteen months Joan was tried as a heretic in a church court at Rouen. She recanted when faced with death by burning, but because she donned men's clothes when led away to begin life imprisonment she was once again accused of heresy. Joan's insistence over her "voices" sent from God and her habit of wearing men's clothing were seen as heretical defiance, and she was sentenced to death and burnt at the stake on May 30, 1431. She was aged only nineteen. Charles VII, who totally deserted her, ordered an inquiry into her trial when he finally took Rouen in 1450.

Joan is also known as the Maid of France or La Pucelle. She is one of the patron saints of France.

Chronology

1412	Born at Domrémy, in Bar, France, January 6
1428	Hears angelic voices telling her to go to the Dauphin and help him regain his kingdom from the English
1429	Meets Dauphin at Chinon. Rescued city of Orléans from being besieged by the English. Witnessed coronation of Dauphin as King Charles VII of France at Rheims. Urged Charles to attack Paris. He refused, but many towns in northern France surrendered to him. In September led troops to Paris but failed to take city
1430	Tries to repel the Burgundians from Compiègne but was captured by John of Luxembourg
1431	Tried for heresy by church court. Burnt at the stake, May 30
1920	Canonized

Gustavus Adolphus

Gustavus Adolphus (1594–1632), King Gustav II of Sweden and leader of the Protestant forces in the Thirty Years' War, was one of the fathers of modern warfare and the founder of the modern Swedish state. He formed the first national conscript army in Europe, and planned his military campaigns on the basis that attack was the best form of defense.

The son of Charles IX, Gustav was groomed in warfare and succeeded to the throne aged sixteen with Sweden engaged in war on three fronts—against Denmark, Russia, and Poland.

He made peace with Denmark, by agreeing to pay huge indemnities, but pursued Swedish campaigns against Russia and Poland, eventually securing big territorial gains in the Baltics, pushing back Russia and neutralizing the threat to his throne from his cousin, Sigismund III, King of Poland, with the 1629 Truce of Altmark. By this time, Gustavus was known as the "Lion of the North."

A New Model Army

■ Gustavus' army was based on permanent conscripts and rigorous training. He was the first commander to use musketeers in three ranks, each firing in turn while the others reloaded.

■ At the Battle of Breitenfeld (1631), Gustavus set a new first in modern warfare when he moved Swedish troops across the field to create a second front in place of a Saxon line that had been broken by the imperial army under Graf von Tilly. A counter-attack personally led by Gustavus won the day for the Swedes.

■ After the battle of Lützen, the Swedish king's body was found under a pile of dead bodies; he was naked, with a bullet hole through his head, a dagger thrust in his side, and another bullet in his back.

At home, Gustavus laid the groundwork of the modern Swedish state, establishing a new supreme court, a permanent civil service with treasury and chancery in Stockholm, and a standing army and navy. He worked in tandem with Axel Oxenstierna, a brilliant chancellor; their constitutional arrangements gave the council of state a permanent role in government and conferred new status to the Riksdag, or parliament. Gustavus did much for education; he permanently funded Uppsala University in Sweden and founded the University of Tartu in Swedish-occupied Estonia, and created the Gymnasia to provide national secondary education. Under Gustavus, Sweden became the most modern and efficiently run state in Europe.

Under Gustavus, Sweden became the most modern and efficiently run state in Europe

Gustavus was at his most innovative as a war leader. Forming the first national conscript army in modern Europe, he emphasized officer education, strict discipline, rigorous training, and the combination of firepower and mobility, till he had forged a formidable fighting force that stands unrivaled between Caesar's legions and Napoleon's "Grande Armée." He always believed that attack was the best form of defense and he created a policy of making his wars pay for themselves.

In 1630 Gustavus rescued the beleaguered Protestant cause in Germany from the Catholic League of the Holy Roman Emperor Ferdinand II, militarily led by the era's two other great

captains, the Habsburg commanders Johann Tserclaes Graf von Tilly and Albrecht von Wallenstein. Gustavus triumphed against them (twice defeating Tilly) in battles that are regarded by military historians as tactical masterpieces. His victory over Tilly at Breitenfeld in 1631 was a landmark in the art of war. Gustavus, seeing his left flank was routed by the imperial army, moved Swedish infantry into the breach, an unprecedented move for the times. In the ensuing months, Gustavus swept all before him as his army pushed into southern Germany, and the following year he beat Tilly again and left him mortally wounded at the Battle of the River Lech. His army was at first checked by Tilly's successor, Wallenstein, at Alte Veste in September 1632 but on November 6 Gustavus attacked Wallenstein's entrenched positions at Lützen, near Leipzig, in Saxony, and again overwhelmed the imperial army. Gustavus himself, however, was shot and killed in a cavalry charge.

He died just a few weeks before his thirty-eighth birthday, but he had made Sweden a major European power, and set new standards for warfare; his victories over the Catholic League assured Protestant survival in Germany and northern Europe.

Chronology

1594	Born at Stockholm, December 9
1611	Becomes King of Sweden October 30
1613	Concludes peace with Denmark
1630	Sweden enters Thirty Years' War
1631	Victory over Tilly at Battle of Breitenfeld
1632	Victory over Tilly at Batle of Lech
1632	Victory and death, Lützen, November 6

Horatio Nelson

Horatio Nelson (1758–1805) won naval victories that gave Britain dominance of the seas for a century. His charisma and the manner of his victories are such that he is known simply as "The Hero," and every year, on Trafalgar Day, the Royal Navy toasts "The Immortal Memory."

Horatio Nelson was the son of a Norfolk parson and went to sea aged twelve. His early years under sail saw him serve in the West Indies, the Arctic, Nicaragua, and in the American War of Independence, suffering much ill health. He was appointed captain in 1779 and married in 1787, only to spend nearly six years unemployed in England before the outbreak of the French Revolutionary Wars.

Nelson shot to fame when serving under Admiral Sir John Jervis at the Battle of Cape St. Vincent on St. Valentine's Day 1797. This battle promised to be inconclusive (as so many of the battles of the period were), until Nelson broke away from the British line of battle—in normal circumstances an unforgivable breach of discipline—so as to cut off the enemy's retreat. He first captured one Spanish ship, which he then used as a stepping-stone, his own ship being unmanageable, to capture a second, the enormous *San Josef.*

Six months later, Nelson lost his right arm in a failed attack in Tenerife. After a period of recuperation, he was given command of a squadron charged with hunting down the fleet with which Napoleon had sailed for Egypt. Nelson eventually tracked them down to the mouth of the Nile, at Aboukir Bay, on the evening of August 1 1798. He launched an immediate attack, sailing both inside and outside the French moorings and obliterating their fleet. The climax of the night-time battle was marked by the gigantic explosion of the French flagship *L'Orient.* It has been said that "a victory so decisive, so overwhelming, was unknown in the annals of modern war."

"England expects that every man will do his duty"

Chronology

1758	Born at Burnham Thorpe, Norfolk, England, on September 29
1771	Goes to sea as a midshipman
1787	Marries Frances Nisbet
1794	Wounded in his right eye at Calvi
1797	Promoted to rear admiral
1797	Battle of Cape St. Vincent, made a Knight of the Bath
1797	Loses right arm at Santa Cruz
1798	Battle of the Nile, created baron
1799	Begins love affair with Emma, Lady Hamilton
1799	Created Duke of Bronte by the King of Naples
1801	Battle of Copenhagen, created viscount
1805	Killed at the Battle of Trafalgar, October 21

Nelson was seriously wounded and spent the next few months at the Sicilian court, where he began his passionate romance with Emma Hamilton, wife of the British ambassador. To this period belongs the most controversial episode of his career, the suppression of the revolution led by Commodore Caracciolo and Caracciolo's execution, for which the King of Sicily conferred upon Nelson the dukedom of Bronte.

Nelson separated from his wife on his return to England in 1800. The following year he was sent under Admiral Hyde Parker to the Baltic and, facing formidable obstacles, defeated the Danes at Copenhagen on April 1 (turning the famous blind eye to a signal ordering him to break off action). The next few years were spent in arduous service, much of it blockading the French fleet at Toulon. After pursuing the

French to the West Indies, he took command of the fleet that was keeping watch on the French and Spanish fleets sheltering in Cadiz. The combined fleet left harbor on October 19 and two days later Nelson, hoisting his celebrated signal "England Expects that Every Man Will Do his Duty," attacked in two columns (an extremely novel strategy for the time). He died from a sniper's bullet at half-past four in the afternoon, just as the complete and overwhelming victory for which he had striven was secured.

The Nelson Touch

■ Nelson's memorandum before the Battle of Trafalgar has been held as a model of management method. It sets out the revolutionary tactics he wished to be followed, while leaving initiative with individual officers, concluding that, if his signals could not be seen, "no captain can do very wrong if he places his ship alongside that of the enemy."

■ As a leader, Nelson relished public recognition and honors. But he was generous to his subordinates, and delegated a good deal of responsibility to his captains. He was admired and loved by those who served under him.

■ Nelson is famous for having only one eye; but he lost only the sight of his right eye, rather than the eye itself—what appears in some portraits to be an eye-patch is in fact a shade to protect his undamaged left eye from strain.

Napoleon Bonaparte

Napoleon Bonaparte (1769–1821) was among the greatest military leaders of all time. He rose from humble origins to become Emperor of France and, for a while, master of Europe.

Born in 1769 in Corsica, Napoleon was commissioned into the French artillery in 1785 and rose rapidly, distinguishing himself at the siege of Toulon (1793), and in dispersing a Royalist uprising in Paris (1795) and conquering North Italy for France (1796–7). On returning from the Egyptian campaign (1798–9), he engineered a coup d'état and became First Consul, and crowned himself Emperor in 1804. After a short-lived peace, Britain provoked a war that lasted from 1803 to 1812. Napoleon knocked out Britain's allies—Austria, Prussia, and Russia—at Austerlitz (1805), Jena (1806), Friedland (1807), and Wagram (1809), but Britain fought on. Napoleon invaded Portugal (1807), Spain (1808), and Russia (1812), to undermine Britain economically, but this led to the turning of the tide; driven from Russia and Spain, Napoleon lost Leipzig (1813) and was forced to abdicate in 1814. Made sovereign of Elba, he escaped to France in 1815 and ruled for a "Hundred Days" before being outnumbered and defeated at Waterloo and banished to St. Helena. He was twice married, to Josephine Beauharnais and Marie-Louise of Austria.

Napoleon inherited from the early post-revolutionary years a French style of warfare—offensive, mobile, ruthless—that confounded opponents. He perfected it through his charismatic leadership and his tactical intelligence. Wellington valued Napoleon's presence on a battlefield at an extra 40,000 men.

"In the long run, the sword is always defeated by spirit"

Napoleon was adept at inspiring from all ranks the devotion and courage he prized. In choosing subordinates he looked for luck, unorthodoxy and aggression ("I only like officers who make war"); they led from the front and died for him in comparatively high numbers.

He never systematized his tactics. "There are no precise or definite rules…everything is a matter of execution." But his hallmarks, daring apart, were rapidity of movement and concentration, and subterfuge, seeking to divide adversaries, or throw them off balance, so as to achieve local superiority.

Austerlitz (1805) was his masterpiece. Feigning weakness on his right he provoked battle and split a larger Russo-Austrian force, then drove up the middle and rolled up the over-extended enemy left.

After 1807, victory came less easily. He resorted more often to frontal assaults, using massed artillery to penetrate the enemy line. Some military historians detect a decline

Chronology

1769	Born in Ajaccio, Corsica, August 15
1785	Commissioned into artillery
1793	Makes name for himself at siege of Toulon
1795	Suppresses Royalist uprising in Paris
1796–7	Victory over Austrians in North Italy
1798	Egyptian campaign
1799	Seizes power in coup and becomes First Consul
1800	Defeats Austrians at Marengo
1804	Crowns himself Emperor
1805	Defeats Austrians and Russians at Austerlitz
1806	Defeats Prussians at Jena
1807	Invades Portugal, begins Peninsular War
1812	Invades Russia
1813	Defeated by Allied force at Leipzig
1814	Abdicates, becomes sovereign of Elba
1815	Escapes to France, defeated at Waterloo, exiled
1821	Dies at Langwood House, St. Helena, May 5

in his powers. But his defensive campaign east of Paris in 1814 was as brilliant in its way as his first campaign in Italy.

In French eyes, Napoleon was also a great administrator. In the run-up to his Consulate it was said of him: "Of all the soldiers, he is the nearest to being a civilian." Possessing a lucid, penetrating brain, tremendous powers of concentration, and unflagging energy, imposing his will came naturally to him. His instincts included thrift, moderation, and social liberalism.

His achievements were many. He reformed the tax system, created the Bank of France, and restored French finances. He drove through the drafting of a Civil Code which has stood the test of time. He reformed the criminal justice system and local administration (creation of the Prefecture). He strengthened higher education. He normalized relations between church and state. He invigorated French agriculture, and had roads, canals, and ports built.

He put France to work, generating a sense of stability and opportunity. Goethe described Napoleon's administrative work as a form of genius.

Napoleon set himself high standards, believing himself driven by noble ideals: love of France, honor, and the Rights of Man. He was courageous, magnanimous in victory, and generous. Austrian statesman Metternich reported him as saying in 1813: "A man such as I am cares little for the lives of a million men," but his treatment of wounded suggests otherwise.

Many (not all) English contemporaries saw him as an autocrat, a parvenu adventurer, a monster of ambition, obsessed with his own glory. But, autocracy apart, this charge-sheet looks exaggerated by snobbery and fear.

His greatest failings—the cause of his downfall—were of judgment. He believed too readily in the loyalty of others; the list of those who let him down is long. He inclined to over-confidence and lacked a sense of his own limits, rendering his strategic vision at times defective.

Specifically, Napoleon miscalculated the consequences of invading Spain and compelling the Bourbons to renounce the Spanish throne. He failed to appreciate how much Germany, Italy, and Holland resented French occupation. He underestimated the risks before and during his Russian campaign. In the peace negotiations of 1813 and 1814 he showed little sense of reality.

It was also characteristic of Napoleon that, after the Battle of Waterloo, he misjudged the British view of him sufficiently to believe that they would welcome him with open arms. They did not.

The Hundred Days

■ After Napoleon's escape from his first period of exile on Elba, March 1815, he returned to France. He crossed the frontier into Belgium on June 15, taking the Prussians by surprise and defeating them at Ligny on June 16. Defeat at Waterloo on June 18, however, meant another period of exile, this time on St. Helena, where he remained until his death on May 5, 1821.

Duke of Wellington

Arthur Wellesley, 1st Duke of Wellington (1769–1852), was one of Britain's greatest military commanders, but he was also one of her worst prime ministers. At a time of peril, when his country most needed victories, this great soldier never lost a battle.

Arthur Wellesley was born in Dublin, the fourth son of an impoverished Anglo-Irish peer. He always denied being Irish, stating that being born in a barn does not make someone a horse. Unsuccessful at any of his schools, including Eton, he ended up in a French military academy in Angers, where he found his metier.

Following his mother's wishes he joined a Highland regiment. His initial rise was largely due to his family's influence, with his brother buying him command of the 33rd Foot Regiment, which, after a campaign in Flanders (1794), he took to India in 1797, where another brother, Richard, was governor general. Wellesley took part in several successful campaigns, including the invasion of Mysore in 1799 and the Battle of Assaye in 1803, which he considered to be the finest of his sixty victories.

Promoted to major general and knighted, he returned home in 1805. The following year he married Lady Katherine Pakenham and was also elected Member of Parliament for Rye. In 1807, largely thanks to family patronage, he was made Chief Secretary of Ireland, and took time off to notch up a victory against the French in Denmark.

In 1808, by now lieutenant general, Wellesley was given command of the British expeditionary force sent to Portugal to aid in their insurrection against the French. The Iberian campaign started well with victories at Roliça and Vimiero. But Wellesley was summoned home to face a court martial (at which he was exonerated) and was therefore away from the Peninsula when Napoleon arrived to take personal command of the French forces, so the two men came face to face for the first and only time at Waterloo.

Wellesley spent six years driving the French from the Peninsula, rarely taking a day's leave. Frequently outnumbered by the huge French forces that were occupying Spain, he employed scorched-earth tactics to deny them territory, used speed and defensive positions to great advantage, and never lost a battle. Talavera (1809), Salamanca (1812), and Vitoria (1813) were among his famous victories. Wellesley showed exemplary leadership; he expected and exacted the best from his men, and he was a harsh disciplinarian when he did not get it. He described his men as "the scum of the earth" but they admired him because he kept them well fed, never unduly risked their lives, and showed personal bravery on the battlefield.

Wellesley crossed the Pyrenees into France to win a further victory at Toulouse before Napoleon abdicated in 1814. By now the Duke of Wellington, he was appointed British ambassador in Paris, and he was representing Britain at the Congress of Vienna when, in March 1815, Napoleon escaped from Elba to launch his final and doomed bid for European supremacy.

Chronology

1769	Born Dublin, Ireland, May 1
1787	Commissioned to 73rd Highlanders
1793	Promoted lieutenant colonel
1794	Campaigns in Holland
1797–1805	Commands army in India
1804	Knighted
1806	Elected MP for Rye
1807	Chief Secretary for Ireland
1808–14	Peninsular War
1814	Created Duke of Wellington
1815	Defeats Napoleon at Battle of Waterloo
1818	Enters Cabinet
1828–31	Prime Minister
1852	Dies at Walmer Castle, Kent, September 14

Wellington assumed command of the Anglo-Allied army in Brussels. This army was made up of a mix of British, Dutch, Belgian, and German soldiers, many of whom were raw recruits. In June 1815 Napoleon marched on Belgium, making for Brussels. On June 16 he simultaneously attacked the Anglo-Allied army at Quatre Bras and the Prussian army under Marshal Blücher at Ligny, routing the latter. Wellington was forced to retreat to the slopes of Mont St-Jean, south of his headquarters at Waterloo.

Only 3 miles (5 km) wide, the battlefield was protected by woods and villages on the flanks, and two well-defended farms in the center. The French attacked at midday on Sunday June 18, but failed to break Wellington's line. The Duke was everywhere on the field, encouraging his men. Prussian general Blücher's troops arrived in the nick of time in the late afternoon to surprise Napoleon and attack his left flank, and by 7 pm the French were routed. After Waterloo, Wellington remained in France for three years as head of the allied army of occupation.

Returning to England and politics, he entered the Cabinet in 1818 and in 1828 he became Prime Minister. In office he changed his opinion on the Irish question, and came to favor Catholic emancipation, saying that the only alternative was conflict. Wellington was less liberal on the question of extending voting rights. He defended rule by the elite and feared the mob—a fear strengthened by riots against unemployment. His opposition to reform caused his popularity to fall to such an extent that crowds gathered at Apsley House, his London home. Wellington's nickname "the Iron Duke" was acquired not from his rigid command of the army, but because of the iron shutters he had installed at his home after it was attacked by mobs. Wellington resigned in 1830. Two years later he joined Robert Peel's administration as Foreign Secretary and later as Leader of the Lords and, following Peel's resignation in 1846, he retired himself.

Wellington died in 1852 and though his political career was distinctly less impressive than his military, nothing can detract from the untarnished glory he earned in England and throughout Europe as the vanquisher of Napoleon.

Key Quotes

■ "I don't know what effect they will have upon the enemy, but by God they frighten me." On seeing his raw recruits arriving in the Peninsula.

■ "By God! I don't think it would have been done if I had not been there." After the Battle of Waterloo, 1815.

■ "An extraordinary affair. I gave them their orders and they wanted to stay and discuss them." After his first Cabinet meeting as Prime Minister.

Wellesley spent six years driving the French from the Peninsula, taking only a few days' leave in the time

Douglas MacArthur

General Douglas MacArthur (1880–1964) was one of the U.S. army's most decorated soldiers. Called out of retirement in World War II to command the forces that defeated the Japanese in the Pacific, he presided over the creation of a new postwar Japan and was commander in chief of Allied forces in the Far East until sacked for insubordination during the Korean War.

Douglas MacArthur was born in 1880 in the U.S. army arsenal barracks at Little Rock, Arkansas, the third son of Arthur MacArthur, later the U.S. army's senior ranking officer. After an irregular education, MacArthur entered West Point in 1889. In 1903, he graduated with the highest honors in his class. As a 2nd lieutenant, he served in the Philippines, and in 1904 he was promoted 1st lieutenant.

In 1906, he was appointed aide to President Theodore Roosevelt. Later, he served as a junior engineering officer and from 1913 as an officer on the general staff. In 1914, he was promoted captain and fought with U.S. troops who occupied Vera Cruz, Mexico, earning a recommendation for the Congressional Medal of Honor.

MacArthur joined the Western front as major in 1915 and by 1917 he had become the U.S. army's youngest divisional commander. He showed conspicuous courage in the trenches. Disdaining both a gas mask and a steel helmet, he led his men over the top armed only with a riding crop. He was wounded twice and decorated nine times for bravery in 1918.

After the war he remained in Europe as part of the force occupying the Rhineland. Returning home, he became the youngest superintendent of West Point and, after two commands in the Philippines, was promoted chief of staff in 1930. He spent five tough years protecting the army's meager resources during the depression. From 1935 to 1941, he served as the military adviser to the Philippines government. He retired from the U.S. army in 1937, but stayed on in Manila as field marshal in the new Philippines army.

"I shall return"

As war clouds gathered, MacArthur was recalled to active service in July 1941 and told to prepare the Philippines' defenses for a Japanese attack. The Japanese landed on December 22 and pushed MacArthur's 130,000 men back into the Baatan Peninsula. On March 11, 1942, on the direct orders of

President Roosevelt, MacArthur reluctantly fled the Philippines, vowing: "I shall return."

From his base in Australia, MacArthur coordinated a series of amphibious invasions to "island hop" U.S. forces back across the Pacific, starting with the capture of New Guinea. He was appointed a five-star general in December 1944, and as Allied Commander of the Pacific he took the Japanese surrender in Yokohama Bay on the battleship Missouri on September 2, 1945.

From 1945 to 1951, as proconsul in Japan, MacArthur directed the demobilization of the Japanese forces, the purging of militarists, the trial and execution of Homma and Yamashita, the restoration of the economy, public health, and education, and the introduction of land reform, women's rights, and the drafting of a liberal constitution. He also astutely preserved the institution of emperor, albeit minus his divine attributes.

When the Korean War started in 1950, MacArthur was given command of the United Nations forces. The North Koreans had pushed across the 38th parallel, the boundary between North and South Korea, captured Seoul, and driven the South Korean forces to the Pusan perimeter on the southeastern tip of the Korean Peninsula. The seventy-year-old MacArthur outflanked the North Korean forces by landing at Fuchon in September, recaptured Seoul, and advanced into North Korea as the North Korean army disintegrated.

Chronology

1880	Born Little Rock on January 26
1903	Graduated West Point with highest honors
1914	Vera Cruz raid: recommended for Congressional Medal
1918	Fighting in France, decorated nine times; promoted general
1919	Superintendent of West Point
1930–35	Army Chief of Staff
1937	Retires from U.S. army
1941	Recalled to arms
1942	Flees to Australia; launches "island hopping" offensive
1943–4	Seizes New Guinea; attacks the Philippines; appointed five-star general in command Pacific Theater
1945	Accepts surrender of Japanese forces on September 2
1945–51	Proconsul of Japan
1950	General in command of UN forces in Korea
1951	Sacked by President Truman; retires into private life
1964	Publishes *Reminiscences*; dies in Washington, D.C. April 5

"Old Soldiers"

■ MacArthur was given a hero's welcome on his return to the United States in 1951, his first trip home since 1937. On April 19 he addressed a joint session of Congress to defend his policy of taking the war to China. He closed his address with the words from an old army ballad, "...old soldiers never die; they just fade away."

■ MacArthur accepted the chairmanship of the Remington Rand Corporation in 1952. Thereafter, he lived a mostly private life in his suite in the Waldorf Astoria Hotel in New York. In 1964, he published his memoirs, *Reminiscences*.

The Chinese had massed north of the Yalu River, the boundary between North Korea and China. MacArthur assured President Truman that the Chinese would not attack. Based on this assurance, Truman allowed MacArthur to drive on toward the Yalu River. However, on November 24 the Chinese attacked and drove MacArthur's troops south of the 38th parallel. MacArthur's counter-attack in February 1951 was inconclusive. MacArthur blamed the restrictions placed upon him; he rejected a policy that aimed merely to restore the prewar boundary along the 38th parallel.

In March 1951, just before Truman was to propose a ceasefire to the North Korean and Chinese leaders, MacArthur issued a public demand that Chinese forces surrender or risk attacks upon their homeland. In April 1951, Truman dismissed MacArthur for insubordination. A ceasefire was negotiated, and the boundary along the 38th parallel was restored.

William Slim

General William Slim (1891–1970) joined the British Army as a private and left as Chief of the Imperial General Staff. He commanded the Fourteenth Army during World War II and was the architect of the British victory over the Japanese in Burma in the face of overwhelming odds. He is widely recognized as one of Britain's finest generals.

Born the son of an iron merchant in Bristol, England, in 1891, Slim volunteered as a private soldier in the Royal Warwickshire Regiment as World War I broke out. He saw action during the abortive Gallipoli landings, where he was wounded so badly that he was invalided out of the army. After persuading the army that he was not so badly wounded after all, he saw action on the Western Front and in Mesopotamia, where he was wounded once again.

At the outbreak of World War II, Slim was in command of the 10th Infantry Brigade, 5th Indian Division, which threw back the Italian invasion of Eritrea and prevented them from entering the Sudan. Wounded again, he recovered to lead the 10th through Syria, Iraq, and Persia, joining up with the Russian army at Tehran. The success of these operations won him the DSO.

Posted to India, Slim was given charge of the two British-Indian divisions retreating from the Japanese invasion in Burma. Outnumbered and outgunned, Slim led a superbly organized retreat almost 1,000 miles (1,610 km) to cross the Chindwin River into India, where he set about reorganizing the exhausted troops. In November 1943 he was given command of the Fourteenth Army, while Lord Louis Mountbatten took control of all Allied ground forces in India. Between them, the two commanders managed to transform a demoralized army into a keen fighting force. After the British XV Corps successfully took on the Japanese in the Arakan, close to the Indian-Burmese border, Allied troops realized that the Japanese army was far from invincible and morale quickly began to rise. When the Japanese Fifteenth Army launched a major offensive into India in March 1944, the British were waiting, at Imphal and Kohima. Aware of the crucial nature of these positions, Slim was determined to hold them at all costs, supplying the encircled 50,000 British troops by air, and massing the 33rd Corps to their rear. In some of the fiercest fighting of the war, Slim pushed the Japanese back out of India. The moment he had been waiting for had arrived; as 1945 opened, Slim and the Fourteenth Army recrossed the Chindwin river, and began the advance into Burma. Unconvinced that the Japanese were giving up, Slim advanced cautiously, realizing that the Japanese were hoping to entice the bulk of his forces into central Burma, where they could be cut off and destroyed by the far from finished Japanese army. In a monumental piece of trickery, using fake radio

Chronology

1891	Born Bristol, England, August 6
1914	Joins Royal Warwickshire Regt. as private
1915	Wounded at Gallipoli
1916–18	Service on the Western Front and Mesopotamia; awarded the Military Cross
1920	Receives his commission; transfers to 6th Gurkha Rifles of the Indian Army
1939	Commands troops in Middle East
1942	Commands British retreat from Burma
1944	March–September, holds off Japanese attacks on Imphal and Kohima
1945	January; leads British advance into Burma; March, captures Mandalay; May 2, fall of Rangoon; victory in Burma.
1953–1960	Governor General of Australia
1970	Dies in London, December 14

"The finest general the Second World War has produced"

Lord Louis Mountbatten on Slim

traffic and dummy headquarters, he fooled the Japanese into believing he was indeed advancing with all speed into the Burmese heartland. As the Japanese waited to spring their trap to the south of Mandalay, however, they found themselves outflanked and outmaneuvered by the Fourteenth. By March 4, Mandalay had been recaptured, and British forces had cut the main railway route south to Meiktila. Slim entered Rangoon on May 2, prompting Lord Louis Mountbatten to remark that "Slim is the finest general the Second World War has produced."

As the Fourteenth continued to mop up Japanese resistance in Burma, and to prepare itself for further fighting elsewhere, the atomic bombs on Hiroshima and Nagasaki brought the surrender of the Japanese. In the chaotic jubilation that followed the end of six years of war, Slim's superhuman efforts in the jungles of Burma slipped from the public awareness, overshadowed by events in Europe and the Pacific, and the Fourteenth became the "Forgotten" once more. Slim went on to become Montgomery's successor as Chief of the Imperial General Staff in 1948, was promoted to Field Marshal, and decorated with the CBE and the KCB. He served as Governor General of Australia from 1953 to 1960, when he was created a viscount. General Slim died in London on December 14, 1970.

"Uncle Bill" in Burma

■ On his arrival in Burma, Slim realized that the common image of the Japanese soldier as "indestructible" was damaging in the extreme to Allied morale. He at once set about rebuilding morale among the troops, giving them proper jungle training and a constant succession of pep talks. The measure of success enjoyed by XV Corps in their incursion into the Arakan in December 1943, coupled with the activities of Orde Wingate's Chindits behind Japanese lines, brought home to the Allies the fact that Japanese soldiers were much like any others, and could be taken on and defeated.

■ Much of Slim's success in rebuilding his troops into the Fourteenth Army stems from his own character. A down-to-earth, approachable man, "Uncle Bill," as he became known throughout the Fourteenth, inspired not only great respect but genuine affection from his subordinate commanders and men, in a way that perhaps no other commander since the days of Nelson and Wellington had achieved.

Dwight D. Eisenhower

Dwight D. ("Ike") Eisenhower (1890–1969) was a professional soldier who began World War II a major and ended it as commander of the greatest amphibious operation in history, with four million men under his command. He was U.S. President from 1953 to 1961.

Born David Dwight Eisenhower (he later reversed the names) in Denison, Texas, this most famous son of Kansas (his family settled in Abilene in 1892) was always set for a career in the military. A Swiss-German Protestant by descent, Eisenhower would epitomize the unglamorous virtues of modesty and meticulousness. Of the 164 members of his 1915 class at West Point, 59 would become generals, a record never surpassed. Eisenhower graduated 61st and began an unspectacular career, training troops in World War I and then serving in the obscurity of the Panama Canal Zone.

In 1925–26, however, he graduated first in a class of 275 at the Command and General Staff School at Fort Leavenworth. Administrative ability then took Eisenhower via the War College, the Office of Assistant Secretary of War, and the Army Industrial College to become aide to General Douglas MacArthur in creating an army for the Philippines. Within a year of Pearl Harbor, Eisenhower had been recalled to Washington and was commanding an Allied invasion of North Africa, followed by equally successful operations in Sicily, Italy, and Normandy.

Eisenhower helped General Marshall to draft a strategy for victory, and it fell to him to implement it. He accepted the surrender of the German army at Rheims on VE Day, commanded the occupation of the defeated foe, and presided over the unification of the U.S. armed forces. He then retired to become President of Columbia University.

Declining presidential nomination in 1948, Eisenhower returned to service as European commander of NATO forces (1950–52) before accepting the Republican ticket in 1952 to win decisively over Adlai Stevenson. Eisenhower's

> *"I hate war as only a soldier who has lived it can"*

Chronology

1890	Born in Denison, Texas, October 14
1909–15	Attends West Point
1917–19	Commands tank training center
1933–5	Aide to General Douglas MacArthur
1941	Assigned to prepare for Allied invasion of Europe
1942	Commands Allied invasion of North Africa
1943	Commands Allied invasions of Sicily and Italy
1944	Appointed Supreme Commander of Allied Expeditionary Force to invade France
1945	War ends in Europe
1953–61	U.S. President
1969	Dies in Washington, D.C., March 28

first presidency matched America's yearning for normality after the radicalism of the Roosevelt era, the strains of war, and the uncertainties of an unexpectedly fragile peace. The nation and its leader enjoyed prosperity and golf. Eisenhower successfully disengaged U.S. forces from Korea, sidestepped the anti-Communist antics of Senator McCarthy, and dutifully enforced the desegregation of schools. Reactive rather than proactive in foreign policy, he committed the United States to resist the spread of Communism into South Vietnam and pressured the UK into abandoning its military intervention in Egypt. Reelected in 1956 by the largest popular vote in U.S. electoral history, Eisenhower supported the Lebanese government against internal rebellion but failed to achieve any significant improvement in relations with the USSR.

A telling cartoon of the day depicted Eisenhower asking his Cabinet what the administration should refrain from doing that day. Subsequent historians were to castigate the thirty-fourth president's tenure of office as an era of drift, indecisiveness, and lost opportunities. The bravura and panache of the following Kennedy administration perhaps made such comparisons irresistible. Despite the image of bridge-playing insouciance, however, Eisenhower put in long hours and enjoyed the exercise of power without needing to parade it. Just as he had successfully managed the egomania of wartime subordinates like Patton and Montgomery, Eisenhower worked effectively with a Congress under Democrat control to promote social reform.

By his caution he used the prestige of a war-winning general to de-escalate tensions abroad. Emollience and patience are qualities not normally associated with the military but they served Eisenhower well. Far more subtle than his critics ever realized, he distrusted any show of brilliance because it created distrust in others. Eisenhower, who had never seen battlefield action in person, managed to wage eight years of peace at the height of the Cold War. A 1962 poll of presidential historians rated him twentieth, at the bottom end of the "average" cohort. By 1995 he was rated ninth, his highest score being for—character.

The Quiet Man

■ Eisenhower was appointed Supreme Commander of the Allied Expeditionary Forces for the invasion of France on December 24, 1943. Less than six months later, on June 6, 1944, he sent a million men in some 4,000 ships across the Channel to Normandy in the biggest amphibious landing in history.
■ By August 25 the Allies had liberated Paris, and, after reversing a fierce German counter-attack in the Ardennes in December, Allied troops crossed the Rhine on March 7, 1945. On May 7 Admiral Karl Dönitz surrendered all German forces to the Allies.
■ It was Harry S. Truman who observed that it was surprising how much could be achieved in politics if one was willing to let someone else take the credit. Few followed this maxim more successfully than Dwight D. Eisenhower.

William Wilberforce

William Wilberforce (1759–1833) was a British statesman and reformer who displayed courage and persistence in leading the movement for the abolition of the slave trade. He presented a bill to Parliament to end the trade in humans no fewer than twelve times before it finally became law.

The son of a wealthy merchant from the English east-coast port of Hull, Wilberforce lost his father when he was a young boy, and was brought up for a time by an aunt, who was a strict Methodist. Her influence left him a strong evangelical. He spent three years at Cambridge University, where he met William Pitt, who would become Britain's youngest ever Prime Minister, and at the age of twenty-one he entered Parliament as a member for his native city, Hull. He changed constituencies in 1784 and became a member for Yorkshire. That year he also converted to Evangelical Christianity, and he became interested in parliamentary and social reform, including issues such as Catholic emancipation (Catholics were still outlawed). A group of Quakers and Prime Minister Pitt persuaded him to take up the cause of the abolition of the slave trade, which had developed on both sides of the Atlantic into a highly profitable business.

British ports like Bristol and Liverpool had built their prosperity on the trade. Ships laden with goods, such as guns and cloth, would sail to West Africa, exchange their wares for slaves, and then transport their human cargo to the West Indies, where they would barter them for sugar, tobacco, rum, and molasses. Apart from this triangular maritime trade, which depended on slaves, people believed that the plantation economies of the Americas and the Caribbean would collapse without their labor. The slave owners would put up a determined fight.

Wilberforce and his religious-minded associates were first called the Saints, and later became known as the Clapham Sect, because they mostly lived and worshiped in the South London suburb of Clapham. Apart from the abolition of slavery, they supported Christian missions, and schools for the poor, and opposed blood sports and gambling.

Wilberforce made his first speech to Parliament against the slave trade on May 12, 1789, and in 1791 he presented his first bill to abolish it, which was defeated by 163 votes to 88. He continued to campaign for it inside Parliament and, together with a group of friends, he helped form the countrywide Anti-Slavery Society. In 1792, he succeeded in getting a bill approved for the gradual abolition of the trade—but with no firm date agreed—and he battled on in vain throughout the 1790s. He tried again in 1804, and in 1805 he managed to get a bill passed in the lower House of Commons, but it was thrown out by the upper chamber, the House of Lords. A final attempt, in 1807, succeeded, and a bill to abolish the slave trade became law on March 25, 1807. Wilberforce was cheered by his supporters in Parliament.

"Thank God I have lived to see the day that England is willing to give £20 million for the abolition of slavery"

Chronology

1759	Born in Hull, England, August 24
1776–9	Studies at Cambridge University
1780	Enters Parliament
1789	Makes first speech against the slave trade
1791	Presents first bill to abolish slave trade
1807	Parliament bans slave trade
1825	Retires from Parliament
1833	Dies, July 29

William Wilberforce

A campaign to abolish slavery altogether continued, although Wilberforce, who switched constituencies again in 1812, becoming a member for Sussex, at first did not agree with this. He believed in gradual abolition, arguing that slaves were not ready to be granted their freedom. He eventually came round to accepting abolition, but had retired from Parliament by the time it was debated. Parliament passed the Slavery Abolition Act in August 1833, a month after his death.

The Abolition of Slavery

■ Slaves were bought and sold down the ages in almost every so-called civilization. The trade was a major business in the eighteenth century, and was accepted on both sides of the Atlantic as normal and legitimate commerce. Slaves were mostly bought in Africa and sold in America.

■ The abolition of the slave trade had some initially unforeseen consequences. Ship's masters caught flouting the law would sometimes have their human cargo thrown overboard, rather than pay the fines for carrying slaves.

■ Wilberforce's strong puritan streak shows up in his description of arriving at St John's College, Cambridge: "I was introduced on the very first night of my arrival to as licentious a set of men as can well be conceived. They drank hard, and their conversation was even worse than their lives."

■ When on his deathbed he heard that the bill for the total abolition of slavery would be passed, and that planters would be heavily compensated, Wilberforce said: "Thank God that I have lived to witness a day in which England is willing to give £20 million for the abolition of slavery."

Frederick Douglass

Frederick Douglass (1818–95) was an escaped slave who campaigned on both sides of the Atlantic with fine oratory for the abolition of slavery, and became the first black citizen to hold high office in the United States government.

Frederick Augustus Washington Bailey was born of a white father and a black slave mother and brought up by his grandmother on a Maryland plantation. Aged eight, he became a house servant to the Auld family in Baltimore, where he received a rudimentary education and learned to read and write. He was put to work as a field hand at the age of sixteen, suffering beatings and deprivations, and in 1836 he made an abortive attempt to escape. After a brief spell in prison, he was hired out as a ship caulker in Baltimore. Two years later he fled to New York, and then to New Bedford, Massachusetts, where he worked as a laborer. To elude slave hunters, he changed his

surname to Douglass, and married his Baltimore sweetheart, Anna Murray.

Douglass made his name, and got his first break, in 1841 when he was invited to speak at an anti-slavery convention in Nantucket, Massachusetts. His natural eloquence and his moving first-hand account of his experiences as a slave propelled him into a new career as agent for the local anti-slavery society. He went on a lecture tour, and became an instant hit as a platform speaker for the abolitionists. He addressed audiences from coast to coast, at times having to contend with rough treatment, particularly from pro-slavery activists.

In 1845 he published an autobiography, *Life and Times of Frederick Douglass*, and, still fearful of recapture, he left the United States for two years on a speaking tour of Britain and Ireland. He returned with enough money to buy his freedom and start his own anti-slavery newspaper, the *North Star*, a weekly which he published out of Rochester, New York, from 1847 to 1860. He also became station master and conductor of the underground railway at Rochester.

Douglass went back to Britain on a second speaking tour in 1859, returning to the United

Truth is of No Color

■ The masthead of the *North Star* proclaimed: "Right is of no sex—Truth is of no color—God is the Father of us all, and we are all Brethren."

■ At public meetings, Douglass was presented as "a recent graduate from the institution of slavery with his diploma on his back."

■ Douglass was impelled to write his autobiography largely because his natural intelligence and eloquence led some people to disbelieve his story as he told it to the assembled meetings up and down the country. His account became a classic in American literature and a major source about life as a slave. Published in 1845 as *Narrative of the Life of Frederick Douglass, an American Slave*, it was a runaway success.

Chronology

1818	Born in Tuckahoe, Maryland, February 7
1836	First escape plan fails; imprisoned
1837	Meets Anna Murray
1838	Escapes to New York; marries Anna Murray; changes name to Frederick Douglass
1841	Speaks at American Anti-Slavery Society meeting; invited to go on lecture tour
1845	Autobiography published; tours Britain
1847	Returns to the United States
1847	Starts the *North Star*
1859	Second lecture tour to Britain
1874	President of the Freedman's Savings and Trust Company
1877	U.S. marshal for District of Columbia
1880	Recorder of deeds for Washington, D.C.
1889	American consul general to Haiti
1891	Resigns post and returns home
1895	Dies in Washington, D.C., February 20

States the following year in time to campaign for Abraham Lincoln. During the Civil War, he sought to promote abolition of slavery as one of the North's primary objectives, and he helped raise two black regiments, the Massachusetts 54th and 55th. He complained personally to President Lincoln over the inferior conditions of black soldiers; they were only on half pay. In the reconstruction following the war, Douglass was a prominent spokesman for former black slaves, and campaigned resolutely for amendments to the U.S. Constitution to give freedmen full civil rights. "Slavery is not abolished until the black man has the ballot," he said.

"Slavery is not abolished until the black man has the ballot"

In 1872, Douglass moved to Washington, and two years later he became President of the Freedman's Savings and Trust Bank—a disastrous move, as it quickly went bankrupt. He subsequently took on political and government posts: U.S. marshal for the District of Columbia, recorder of deeds, and, from 1889 to 1891, U.S. minister and consul general in Haiti. He died in Washington in 1895.

Emmeline Pankhurst

Emmeline Pankhurst (1858–1928) was a militant leader of the British women's suffrage movement, which campaigned for women's right to vote. She believed in direct action—something shocking for the age—and fought passionately for women's rights throughout her life. Imprisoned many times, and enduring numerous hunger strikes, she died just two weeks before the British Parliament gave equal voting rights to women.

Emmeline Pankhurst was born in Manchester, England, the daughter of a successful businessman. In an age before universal suffrage, her parents, the Gouldens, were supporters of the vote reform movement, and Emmeline was taken to a women's suffrage meeting by her mother when she was only thirteen. After early schooling in Manchester she was sent aged fifteen to Paris for four years. Her French headmistress believed that girls should have a similar education to boys, including science and bookkeeping as well as embroidery.

When she returned to Manchester in 1878 she met Richard Pankhurst, a lawyer and keen supporter of women's suffrage. Pankhurst had helped to draft a bill that later became the Married Women's Property Act (1882), which for the first time enabled married women to control their property and earnings. In spite of an age difference of twenty-four years, Richard and Emmeline married in 1879, and had four children. Together they helped form the Women's Franchise League in 1889, and switched their allegiance to the new Labour Party in the hopes that it would further their cause.

Emmeline Pankhurst died just two weeks before the British Parliament gave women the vote

In 1895 Mrs Pankhurst became a Poor Law Guardian. She was shocked by how inmates in workhouses—the elderly, the very young, but particularly women—were treated, and felt more strongly than ever that women's suffrage was the only way by which injustices like these could be eradicated.

Disillusioned by existing women's political organizations, Mrs Pankhurst founded the Women's Social and Political Union (WSPU) in 1903 and encouraged working-class women to join. A lack of interest by the media forced the WSPU to use radical methods—direct action—to attract attention. In 1905 Mrs Pankhurst's daughter, Christabel, and Annie Kenney heckled a government minister. They were charged with

Chronology

1858	Born Emmeline Goulden, in Manchester, July 14
1872	Aged thirteen, goes with mother to women's suffrage meeting
1872–76	Schooled in Paris
1876	Works for women's suffrage movement and meets future husband, a radical barrister
1889	Helps found Women's Franchise League
1892	Leaves Liberals; joins Labour Party
1903	With daughter Christabel forms Women's Social and Political Union (WSPU)
1905	Demonstrations by Mrs Pankhurst and members of WSPU at House of Commons
1907–9	Arrested and imprisoned
1917	Women's Party formed
1917	Visits Russia, lives in USA, Canada
1925	Returns to England; joins Conservatives
1928	Dies June 14

Emmeline Pankhurst

assault, and on refusing to pay a fine were imprisoned. This defiance by two respectable women shocked Edwardian England. By 1907 Mrs Pankhurst had joined her daughters in London. She was jailed repeatedly for her violent demonstrations, but her example, and her captivating public speaking, inspired other women to press for the vote.

During World War I the WSPU suspended their militancy, but Mrs Pankhurst, reflecting the new realities of women working in munitions factories, turned her energies to campaigning for trade unions to allow women into male-dominated industries. Then in 1917 she and her daughter Christabel formed the Women's Party. They advocated "equal pay for equal work, equal marriage and divorce laws, the same rights over children for both parents, equality of rights and opportunities in public service, and a system of maternity benefits." Mrs Pankhurst visited revolutionary Russia after the war, and lectured in the United States and Canada. On her return to England in 1925 she again switched party, and became a Conservative parliamentary candidate for the East End of London, shocking another daughter, Sylvia, who was staunchly socialist.

"Deeds Not Words"

■ "Deeds, not words" was the motto of the Women's Social and Political Union (WSPU) founded by Mrs Pankhurst in 1903. It was no idle boast: Emmeline Pankhurst endured ten hunger strikes during an eighteen-month period, when she was in her fifties.

■ She recalled hearing her father say when she was a child, "What a pity she wasn't born a lad."

■ "There can be no doubt about the singleness of her aim and the remarkable strength and nobility of her character...The end she had in view was the emancipation of women from what she believed, with passionate sincerity, to be a condition of harmful subjection." (Obituary of Mrs Pankhurst in *The Times*.)

A bill giving women equal voting rights with men became law, thanks to Mrs Pankhurst's single-minded inspiration and courage, just two weeks after she died on June 14, 1928.

Martin Luther King Jr.

Martin Luther King Jr. (1929–68) was a Baptist Church minister who gave voice to America's blacks in the 1950s and 1960s and led a nonviolent civil rights movement with magnetic eloquence, immortalized in four words of a speech: "I have a dream." He was assassinated by a white man.

Born in Atlanta, Georgia, the son and grandson of Baptist Church ministers, King was a precocious student and had a BA in sociology aged nineteen, a Bachelor of Divinity at twenty-two and a PhD from Boston University in philosophy and theology at twenty-six. He was ordained a Baptist Church minister in 1948 while still at college.

His first full-time ministry was as pastor from 1954 to 1959 at Dexter Avenue Baptist Church in Montgomery, Alabama, America's "deep South," where discrimination against blacks was still institutionalized. It was the arrest in 1955 of a black seamstress, Rosa Parks, for refusing to give up a "whites only" seat in a bus in Montgomery that transformed King's life.

He took up the struggle, determined to emulate his hero, Mahatma Gandhi, who had humbled the British Empire and gained Indian independence through nonviolent protest. King was elected president of the Montgomery Improvement Association, which organized a boycott of the Montgomery buses for 381 days. Protesters were arrested and beaten and King's home was dynamited, but they offered no resistance and the boycott ended in total victory when the Supreme Court outlawed all segregated public transport.

"I have been to the mountain top and I have seen the Promised Land"

King emerged from the protest as a pivotal figure in the civil rights movement, and was elected president of the Southern Christian Leadership Conference, which gave him a national platform from which to speak out against the continued and widespread discrimination against blacks. He became a prominent

A Great Communicator

■ Among King's speeches and articles, his Letter from Birmingham Jail ranks as one of the most compelling. He wrote it in May 1963 after being arrested, along with 3,300 other peaceful protesters, by white police, who had set upon them with dogs, fire hoses, and batons. "We know through painful experience that freedom is never voluntarily given by the oppressor," he wrote. "It must be demanded by the oppressed."

■ In his most famous speech, the address at the Lincoln Memorial of August 28, 1963, he said: "I have a dream that my four children will one day live in a nation where they will not be judged by the color of their skin but by the content of their character."

■ Some 100,000 attended his funeral in Atlanta. His killer, escaped convict James Earl Ray, was sentenced to ninety-nine years in jail.

campaigner both at home and abroad, and his speeches and sermons stirred the nation's conscience and gave blacks a new sense of identity and self-worth. In 1963 he organized a massive civil rights campaign in Birmingham, Alabama, in which 3,300 protesters, including King, were arrested, and he led the historic march in Washington on August 28, 1963 when he delivered his "I have a dream" speech. He also campaigned vigorously against the Vietnam War. Despite critics who demanded more radical action, King never tired of turning the other

cheek, and he stuck to nonviolent protest, such as sit-ins and protest marches. He was arrested no fewer than thirty times, and he was freed on one occasion in 1960 at the behest of John F. Kennedy on the eve of the presidential election. The gesture swung black votes behind Kennedy.

The pressures of leading the civil rights movement forced King to give up his full-time pastorate in 1959, and he took on instead the less demanding role of co-pastor to his father at Ebenezer Baptist Church in Atlanta. He was awarded the Nobel Peace Prize in 1964.

In the last sermon he delivered, on the eve of his assassination, he seemed to foreshadow his death. He said he had "been to the mountain top and seen the Promised Land."

Chronology

1929	Born in Atlanta, Georgia, January 15
1948	Graduates with BA in sociology
1948	Ordained Baptist Church minister
1951	Bachelor of Divinity
1953	Marries Coretta Scott (four children)
1955	Doctorate from Boston University
1954–9	Pastor in Montgomery, Alabama
1955–6	Montgomery bus boycott
1956	Southern Christian Leadership Conference
1960–68	Co-pastor at Ebenezer Baptist Church
1968	Assassinated in Memphis, April 4

King was shot dead the next day while standing on a motel balcony in Memphis, Tennessee. He and the ideals he stood for are commemorated each year in the United States by a national public holiday, on the third Monday of January.

Thomas Jefferson

In the epitaph he wrote for himself, Thomas Jefferson (1743–1826) recorded that he had drafted America's Declaration of Independence and the Virginia Statute for Religious Freedom and had founded the University of Virginia—but omitted to mention that he had served two terms as President of the United States. An aristocratic revolutionary, cultured and learned, Jefferson was a brilliant American standard bearer of the Enlightenment.

The son of a prosperous Virginian plantation owner and educated in law, Jefferson entered politics at twenty-six to become an early activist in the struggle against British rule over the American colonies. His assertive pamphlet, "A Summary View of the Rights of British America" (1774), made him an obvious choice to lead the drafting of the rebellious colonists' Declaration of Independence in 1776. Jefferson's tenure of office as governor of his native state at the height of the revolutionary war was overshadowed by charges of incompetence and cowardice in the conduct of its defense. Although he was subsequently exonerated, the experience left him embittered. Coupled with the death of his wife in 1782, this may explain his willingness to serve the newly independent nation next in an overseas posting.

Jefferson's legislative legacy to Virginia included a commitment to complete religious freedom, which critics took as a deist's swipe at Christianity, and the abolition of entail and primogeniture to prevent the emergence of a "pseudoaristocracy." Jefferson's eloquent and much-quoted condemnations of slavery (the existence of which in America he blamed on the British monarchy) did not, however, cut any ice with fellow-members of Virginia's "plantocracy" nor prevent him from remaining a substantial slave owner to the end of his life. Although he was instrumental in preventing the extension of slavery to the west and foresaw its inevitable abolition, as it was inconsistent with a constitution founded in liberty, Jefferson believed that abolition should be accompanied by the deportation of former slaves.

"We are resolved with one mind to die as free men rather than live as slaves"

Ambassadorial duties in Paris precluded Jefferson from participating in the making of the new nation's constitution, and he deplored its failure to include a bill of rights or limitation on the number of terms a president could hold office. While abroad, Jefferson had only limited success in promoting American trade, finding Europeans largely ignorant of its potential, and managing to sign a commercial treaty only with Prussia. As a first-hand observer of the French Revolution

Chronology

1743	Born at Shadwell, Albemarle Co., Virginia, April 13
1769	Elected to Virginia House of Burgesses
1770	Starts building his mansion, Monticello, in Charlottesville
1779–81	Governor of Virginia
1790–93	Secretary of State
1785–9	Serves as American Minister to France
1796–1800	Vice President
1797–1815	President of the American Philosophical Society
1801–9	President of the United States
1803	Louisiana Purchase
1825	University of Virginia inaugurated
1826	Dies on July 4
1943	Jefferson Monument inaugurated by Franklin D. Roosevelt in Washington, D.C.

he was, and remained, repelled by its arbitrary cruelty and excessive violence, although supportive of its aims. Paradoxically he thought the French incapable of republican government and believed that they should adopt a constitutional monarchy like Britain.

Serving as the first Secretary of State under Washington and then as Vice President under John Adams, Jefferson came to head the emerging agrarianist Republican Party, which opposed the Federalists and Alexander Hamilton's favor for commercial and urban interests. As the nation's 3rd President, Jefferson lived in self-conscious austerity, reflected in his reduction of taxes and military spending. This was offset by a vision of America as a continental power, which led him to dispatch Lewis and Clark on a transcontinental odyssey of exploration and to undertake the

An Autodidact

■ Jefferson was a life-long learner. He grew up intensely interested in botany, geology, cartography, and exploration, and with a love of Latin and Greek. He was widely read in history, philosophy, and literature and was a keen scientist. He designed his own home, Monticello.

■ A technophile in the tradition of Benjamin Franklin, Jefferson also invented the dumbwaiter, a swivel chair, and America's decimal system of coinage.

■ His 1775 Declaration on Taking Up Arms sought to justify armed resistance by the colonists against Great Britain. "Our cause is just. Our union is perfect," Jefferson wrote. "The arms we have been compelled by our enemies to assume, we will, in defiance of every hazard, with unabating firmness and perseverance of our liberties, employ for the preservation of our liberties; being with one mind resolved to die free men rather than to live slaves."

■ The purchase of Louisiana from France in 1803 gave America all the western land drained by the Missouri and Mississippi rivers.

Louisiana Purchase, which doubled the nation's territory in size.

During his second term of office Jefferson ordered a ban on foreign trade to extricate his country from potential involvement in the war between Britain and France. Deeply unpopular with mercantile and maritime interests, his Embargo Act was repealed in 1809 as he withdrew from office.

Unlike Washington, Jefferson enjoyed a lengthy retirement, devoted to the indulgence of his many cultural interests but chiefly to the creation of the University of Virginia, whose buildings and curriculum were both designed by him. The "Sage of Monticello" died on the fiftieth anniversary of the Declaration of Independence.

Toussaint L'Ouverture

François Dominique Toussaint L'Ouverture (1743–1803) was a black slave who led a rebellion that gave birth to Haiti, which in 1804 became the first independent nation in the Caribbean. Although he died in prison before independence was finally achieved, this self-educated slave had effectively outwitted Britain, Spain, and the France of Napoleon Bonaparte.

In 1789 the French colony of Saint-Domingue, the western half of the island of Hispaniola that became Haiti, was one of the most profitable real estates in the world. Its sugar plantations supplied two-thirds of France's overseas trade—all produced by slaves. The French Revolution that year sent shockwaves across the Atlantic, even dividing the whites, and two years later the slaves rebelled en masse.

Toussaint was one of those fortunate slaves who worked for a humane master, as a livestock handler, coachman, and house servant. He was self-educated, intelligent, and energetic, and a devout Catholic. At the outbreak of the uprising in August 1781, Toussaint first ensured the safety of his master's family. He then joined the rebel forces and quickly made his mark with strategic and tactical planning, skills derived from his reading of history. He became a master of guerrilla warfare, and under his leadership the rebels achieved a string of military successes, initially in alliance with France's enemies—Britain and Spain. The Spanish of Santo Domingo controlled the eastern two-thirds of the island of Hispaniola.

But on May 6, 1794, and by now virtually in sole command of the rebels, Toussaint made a

Black Napoleon

■ Toussaint, sometimes known as the "Black Napoleon" or the "Precursor," was given the name L'Ouverture—The Opening—in 1793 after his lightning military successes against the French.

■ Napoleon remained unrepentant about his treatment of Toussaint. "What could the death of one wretched negro mean to me?" he said many years later, when he himself was in exile in Saint Helena.

momentous decision and switched his allegiance back to France. He appears to have been prompted by the decision of the French National Assembly to abolish slavery— emancipation was his primary goal at that stage—and by fears that Spain and Britain would go back on their word and reinstate slavery. Winning seven battles in seven days, Toussaint's soldiers gained control of almost all the island.

Back under French protection, Toussaint was promoted general in 1797. He became lieutenant governor of Saint-Domingue in 1796, and he was later made commander in chief of all French forces on the island. But he was now harboring greater ambitions—to establish an autonomous state under black rule. The U.S. President John Adams, leading an independent but still fledgling nation, sent help, and the last vestiges of French mixed race forces were driven out of Saint-Domingue in late 1800. The following year, Toussaint liberated Spanish Santo Domingo and freed the slaves there.

He now held sway over the whole of Hispaniola, and he had a constitution drawn up that made him governor general for life. He applied his dictatorial powers to restoring order and getting the plantations back to full production.

neglect in the freezing dungeons of Fort de Joux in the Jura Mountains.

Six months later, Napoleon—by now back at war in Europe—signed away Louisiana, bringing French ambitions in the western hemisphere to an end. He abandoned Haiti, and the era of French colonial rule was over.

Winning seven battles in seven days, Toussaint's soldiers gained control of almost all Hispaniola

Trouble, however, was brewing for him back in Paris where Napoleon still regarded Saint-Domingue as essential to the exploitation of his North American territory of Louisiana. Napoleon dispatched his brother-in-law, General Charles Leclerc, to retake the island at the head of a 20,000-strong force. Toussaint was defeated and surrendered to Leclerc on May 5, 1802. He was at first well looked after and assured of his freedom. But, under orders from Napoleon, he was seized a few weeks later and transported back to France, where he died of starvation and

Chronology

1743	Born in Saint-Domingue (Haiti)
1789	French Revolution
1791	Haitian slave revolt
1794	Toussaint switches allegiance back to France
1800	Toussaint controls Saint-Domingue
1801	Toussaint overruns Santo Domingo
1802	Toussaint surrenders to General Leclerc
1803	Dies in Fort de Joux, Jura Mountains, April 7
1804	Haiti becomes an independent republic

José de San Martín

José de San Martín (1778–1850) was one of the principal military leaders in the South American wars of independence against Spain, and is hailed as the liberator of his native Argentina, and of Chile and Peru.

Born of Spanish parents in Yapeyú, on the banks of the mighty Uruguay River in northern Argentina, San Martín moved to Spain as a six-year-old boy to complete his education. He enlisted in the Murcia infantry regiment in 1789—the year of the French Revolution— and spent the next twenty years serving under Spanish colors, fighting against the Moors, the British, the Portuguese, and finally the French. He resigned his commission in 1811, and the following year, after spending time in London, he returned to Buenos Aires, where he married a local girl, Maria Escalada. He found the continent in ferment; Napoleon's invasion of Spain had unsettled her South American colonies and set off a chain reaction of independence movements. San Martín, possibly also influenced by the Latin American revolutionaries he had met in London, was soon involved in one—the Lautaro Lodge.

The fledgling government in Buenos Aires welcomed San Martín, commissioned him as a lieutenant colonel, and put him in charge of a new regiment of mounted grenadiers. The regiment beat a loyalist force near the ravines of San Lorenzo on the River Paraná in its first engagement in 1813.

San Martín took control of the northern army in 1814. By now he was committed to a total break with Spain, but he realized that the only way to make Argentina secure was to drive the Spanish out of neighboring Chile and then conquer Peru. In a masterstroke, he led an army of 4,000 men and horses across the Andes and, on February 12, 1817, surprised and crushed the Spanish at the Battle of Chacabuco. Some days later his army entered Santiago where he was offered the presidency of the new nation of Chile, an offer he declined in favor of his lieutenant, the Chilean general Bernardo O'Higgins.

Early in 1818, the Spanish launched a counter-attack, but San Martín inflicted a decisive defeat

San Martín would display a distinct lack of political ambition when he declined the Chilean presidency

Crossing the Andes

■ San Martín's crossing of the Andes has been compared to Hannibal's feat in leading an army over the Alps. His skill and leadership enabled his men to negotiate passes more than 13,000 feet (4,000 m) above sea level.

■ What happened at Guayaquil? The most likely answer is that Bolívar persuaded San Martín that his army alone was powerful enough to finish off the job. Bolívar was politically far more ambitious; he became president of two countries and had a third named after him, while San Martín displayed a distinct lack of political ambition when he declined the Chilean presidency. Did he sacrifice his career for the sake of South American independence?

■ San Martín left Buenos Aires for the last time in 1824, following the death of his wife. He died more than a quarter of a century later in 1850 in the French Channel port of Boulogne-sur-Mer.

on them at the Battle of Maipú—his most celebrated victory.

San Martín now turned his attention to attacking Peru, and, in his next stroke of genius, he organized the rebels to put together a navy with which to launch a sea-borne assault. With British admiral Lord Cochrane in command, the motley naval force sailed from Valparaiso in August 1820; less than a year later San Martín had taken the capital Lima. He proclaimed the independence of Peru and was appointed protector of the country. The Spanish, meanwhile, had retreated to the Andean foothills.

What happened next has never been clear. But San Martín had a meeting with his fellow Latin American revolutionary, Simón Bolívar, whose armies had been fighting the Spanish to liberate the northern provinces of South America. The meeting between the two "liberators" took place at Guayaquil on July 26, 1822, and after it San Martín resigned his position and withdrew from public life. He left Bolívar to complete the conquest of Peru and, following the death of his wife in 1824, left Latin America to spend the remainder of his life in retirement in Europe.

Chronology	
1778	Born in Yapeyú, Argentina, February 25
1786	Moved to Spain
1789	Joined Murcia regiment in Spanish army
1812	Returned to Buenos Aires
1817	Crossed Andes, victory at Chacabuco, Chile
1818	Battle of Maipú, April 5
1821	Entered Lima, proclaimed Peru's independence
1822	Meeting with Simon Bolívar in Guayaquil
1850	Died in Boulogne-sur-Mer, August 17

Simón Bolívar

Simón Bolívar (1783–1830) was one of South America's greatest generals, and his victories over the Spanish won independence for Bolivia, Colombia, Ecuador, Peru, and Venezuela. Bolívar is called El Liberator (The Liberator) and the "George Washington of South America."

Simón Bolívar was born into a prosperous and powerful colonial family in 1783, in Caracas, Venezuela. His parents died when he was a child, and he was educated at home by tutors and guardians, and inherited a fortune. As a young man, he traveled in Europe, where he married a Spanish aristocrat, and came into direct contact with the new ideas of the Age of Enlightenment and watched enthralled and amazed as Napoleon consolidated his hold over the old order in Europe.

Shortly after returning to Venezuela, Bolívar's new wife died, and her death seems to have had a dramatic effect. This impulsive, passionate man now threw himself into political and military action. He returned to Europe for a few years and came back to Venezuela, via the newly freed United States, to find his country about to be torn apart by Napoleon's invasion of Spain. To whom would the Venezuelans now owe their allegiance—the usurper Joseph Bonaparte or the deposed King Ferdinand VII of Spain?

Chronology

1783	Born in Caracas, July 24
1799	Traveled to Europe for first time
1811	Revolt in Venezuela
1813	Captured and lost Caracas
1814	Captured and lost Bogotá
1819	Captured Angostura
1819	Battle of Boyacá, elected President of Colombia
1824	Elected President of Bolivia
1825	Elected President of Peru
1830	Abandons power; dies near Santa Marta, Colombia, December 17

Bolívar joined a group of patriots and they dispatched him to Britain to seek help. On July 5 Venezuela became the first of Spain's American colonies to declare independence. Bolívar was given command of the strategic coastal town of Puerto Cabello, but he bungled its defense and the First Venezuelan Republic collapsed, and he fled the country to Colombia. Here he issued his Cartagena Manifesto, a call to arms against the Spanish occupation.

He returned to Venezuela the following year at the head of a larger patriot army, and, by now a seasoned campaigner and expert in guerrilla-style surprise attacks, he swept all before him to recapture Caracas in August 1813 and establish the Second Republic, with himself as dictator. But it did not last long; the Spaniards launched a ferocious counter-offensive to retake the city, and the following year Bolívar suffered a similar setback, first capturing and then losing Bogotá.

Bolívar was, however, beginning to learn the most important lesson of his struggle against Spanish rule; with barely a few thousand men under his command, he needed the support of local landlords and their horsemen. He turned the tide when he began to rally them to the cause of independence. From Jamaica he wrote a second manifesto and meanwhile, with the backing of newly independent Haiti, he gathered a new force that included English and Irish mercenary veterans from the Napoleonic wars. He changed tactics, and secured a base in the Orinoco region, at Angostura (now Ciudad Bolívar). From here, on December 17, 1819, he proclaimed the Republic of Colombia (now Ecuador, Colombia, Panama, and Venezuela), and became its first president. He now led his army of fewer than 2,500 men on one of the most daring attacks in military history—over flood-swept plains and the

Bolívar began to turn the tide of war when he rallied local landlords to the cause of independence

Destiny Calls

■ It was on a trip to Rome that Bolívar first determined his destiny; standing on the Monte Sacro he made a vow to liberate his country from Spanish rule.

■ Bolívar's dream of a united Latin America never became a reality. He called a congress in Panama in 1826 to discuss a confederation of Spanish American countries, but only Colombia, Peru, Mexico, and the Central American states turned up.

■ The second love of Bolívar's life was Manuela Sáenz, an ardent revolutionary, whom he met in Quito. She saved him from an assassin's dagger in 1828.

ice-covered Andes—and surprised the Spanish at Boyacá on August 7, 1819. Three days later he entered Bogotá.

Venezuela was finally freed from Spanish rule two years later at the Battle of Carabobo, and Bolívar then set about liberating Ecuador and completing the conquest of Peru, together with his trusted General Antonio José de Sucre, at the Battle of Ayacucho on December 9, 1824. The new state of Bolivia, named in his honor, was established the following year. He now controlled more than half the continent.

But Bolívar was not successful as a government leader, and his vision of Grand Colombia gradually fell apart, as one by one the countries he had freed declared their independence from his increasingly autocratic rule. By 1828 Bolívar was left with only Colombia and, with failing health, he resigned in 1830, and died of tuberculosis, a broken man.

Chief Joseph

Chief Joseph (1840–1904) of the Nez Perce tribe was one of the leaders of the Native American resistance to white encroachment in the western United States, and led his people on an epic but ultimately doomed march to seek sanctuary in British-ruled Canada.

Born with the Indian name In-Mut-Too-Yah-Lat-Lat (Thunder Coming Up over the Land from the Water), Chief Joseph was the son of a Christian convert. Educated in a mission school, he succeeded his father as chief of the Nez Perce in 1873. Although the powerful tribe had been initially on friendly terms with the new settlers, the increasing white encroachments into the Pacific Northwest region led some native leaders to query the validity of land treaties made with the U.S. government, on the grounds that the chiefs responsible for the agreements did not faithfully represent tribal interests. The Stevens Treaty negotiated in 1855 had provided for a large reservation in Oregon and Idaho but, when gold was discovered in Oregon in 1863, nine-tenths of the relevant territory was demanded back. Neither Chief Joseph nor his father had been a party to the latter negotiation. Hostilities broke out in 1877 after the U.S. government forced the reluctant Nez Perce to leave their Wallowa Valley homeland in Oregon and move to Idaho.

"Hear me, my chiefs, my heart is sick and sad. From where the sun now stands, I will fight no more forever"

Chief Joseph had initially assented but he reassessed his options when a band of his braves killed a party of whites. Fearing army retaliation, he determined to lead some 300 warriors and their families to safety across the Canadian border. Between June 17 and September 30 the refugees fled over 1,400 miles (2,250 km) from Oregon through Washington and Idaho into Montana, outmaneuvering a pursuing force of regular soldiers and Indian auxiliaries at least ten times their number, and frustrating it in four major rearguard actions and numerous smaller skirmishes. Chief Joseph's role was primarily one of leadership, rather than of direct military command. Although American journalists were swift to dub him "the Red Napoleon," his own immediate followers were led by his younger brother Olikut, and strategic direction was given by a chief called Looking-Glass (1832–77), who had fled the Idaho reservation to place himself at Chief Joseph's service. The dramatic tribal odyssey won widespread admiration not only for its leader's skill and inspirational example, but also for his evident concern for his most vulnerable followers, his humanity toward

A Dignified Surrender

After a five-day battle in the Bear Paw Mountains, Chief Joseph surrendered on October 5, 1877 with these words:

■ "I am tired of fighting. Our chiefs are killed; Looking-Glass is dead, Ta-Hool-Hool-Shute is dead. The old men are all dead. It is the young men who say yes or no. He who led on the young men is dead. It is cold, and we have no blankets; the little children are freezing to death. My people, some of them have run away to the hills and have no blankets, no food. No one knows where they are, perhaps freezing to death. I want to have time to look for my children and see how many of them I can find. Maybe I can find them among the dead. Hear me, my chiefs, I am tired; my heart is sick and sad. From where the sun now stands I will fight no more forever."

Chronology

1840	Born in the Wallowa Valley, eastern Oregon Territory
1877	Leads 1,400-mile (2,250-km) fighting flight to the Canadian border
1879	Pleads unsuccessfully with President Rutherford B. Hayes
1903	Pleads unsuccessfully with President Theodore Roosevelt
1904	Dies September 21 on the Colville Reservation, Washington

captured enemies, and his integrity in purchasing rather than plundering supplies en route.

Finally surrounded in the Bear Paw Mountains, less than 40 miles (65 km) from the border and deliverance, after a five-day siege Chief Joseph surrendered his people to the custody of the pursuit force commander General Nelson Miles with words of haunting melancholy—"I am tired of fighting. Our chiefs are killed."

Several of his war chiefs who had not been killed in combat did succeed in escaping to Canada. Dispatched initially to a barren tract of Oklahoma, where many sickened and died, the rest of Chief Joseph's surviving followers were

in 1885 allowed to relocate to a reservation in the state of Washington. Chief Joseph himself made two journeys to Washington, D.C. to plead in person with presidents that his people might return to their native homeland valley. He received fair words but no restitution.

Theodor Herzl

Theodor Herzl (1860–1904) was the founder of Zionism, the movement to establish a Jewish homeland in Palestine. After a congress of Zionists in Basle in 1897 he became first president of the World Zionist Organization. Within fifty years of his death, the state of Israel was founded.

Theodore Herzl was born in Budapest, Hungary, and brought up in the liberal spirit of the German Jewish middle class, appreciating secular culture. He left his secondary school because of its anti-Semitic atmosphere, switching in 1875 to a school where the majority of pupils were Jewish. His family moved to Vienna in 1882, and although Herzl was awarded a doctorate of law by the University of Vienna in 1884, he decided to concentrate on journalism and writing plays. He married the daughter of a wealthy Viennese Jewish businessman in 1889, and in 1891 was sent to Paris as correspondent for the leading Viennese newspaper *Neue Freie Presse*. He was shocked by anti-Semitism in France, and his experiences as a journalist there convinced him that the answer for Jews was not to assimilate into the countries where they were living, but to organize themselves on an international level and emigrate to their own state.

The wave of anti-Semitism that swept France during the Dreyfus Affair in 1894, in which a Jewish officer was unjustly accused of spying for the Germans, only reinforced his views. Herzl concluded that anti-Semitism was so deeply rooted in society that it would not be overcome by assimilation. He wrote a pamphlet *Der Judenstaat* (The Jewish State) in 1896, stating that the Jewish problem was a national, not just an individual one, and that the solution was for the international powers to agree to a Jewish state. He was not the first to have these ideas: Judah Alkalai (1798–1878), a Sephardic rabbi from Croatia who had traveled all over Europe founding organizations persuading Jews to return to Israel, had helped to pave the way.

Herzl's ideal Jewish state was planned as a pluralist, neutral, peace-seeking, secular one

Herzl's ideal Jewish state was planned as a pluralist, neutral, peace-seeking, secular one, where socialist cooperative schemes would help to develop the land.

Influential Jews such as Baron Hirsch and Baron Rothschild were sceptical, but ordinary East European Jews were enthusiastic, and the First Zionist Congress met in Basle with some 200 delegates in August 1897. This first meeting of Jews on a secular and national level adopted the Basle Program recognizing the Zionist movement and passed the motion "Zionism seeks to establish a home for the Jewish people in Palestine secured under public law." The international Zionist movement then met every year, moving its center in 1936 to Jerusalem.

Chronology

1860	Born Budapest on May 2
1878	Family moves to Vienna
1882	Studies law at the University of Vienna
1884	Awarded a doctorate of law; starts writing
1894	In Paris during Dreyfus Affair
1897	First Zionist Congress in Basle, Switzerland
1898	Travels to Ottoman Empire and Palestine
1903	Visits Russia and England
1904	Dies of pneumonia in Edlach, Austria, July 3

Herzl was indefatigable in his efforts to persuade the great powers to his point of view, traveling to the then Ottoman-ruled Palestine, Turkey, England, and Russia. The ultimate aim of Zionism was the establishment of a Jewish state in Palestine, but when Britain proposed Uganda in east Africa as a home for the Jews, Herzl felt it could be a temporary alternative for Russian Jews who were suffering persecution. This led to uproar in the Zionist Congress of 1903, and the rejection of Uganda as a Jewish homeland by the 1905 Congress.

By the time Herzl died aged 44 in Vienna in 1904, Zionism was a budding force in world politics, and less than fifty years later the State of Israel was an established fact.

A Life for Zionism

■ Herzl wrote in his diary after the First Zionist Congress of 1897: "At Basle, I founded the Jewish state. If I were to say this today, I would be greeted by universal laughter. In five years, perhaps, and certainly in fifty, everyone will see it."

■ Herzl's phrase "If you will, it is no fairytale" became the motto of the Zionist movement.

■ His name lives on in the first Hebrew grammar school—Herzlia—to be founded in Tel Aviv, and in the town of Herzliya, north of Tel Aviv, as well as in forests and streets throughout Israel. He was reburied on a hill known as Mount Herzl near Jerusalem in 1949, shortly after the foundation of the state of Israel.

Kemal Atatürk

Mustafa Kemal Atatürk (1881–1938) was a war hero who created the secular republic of Turkey from the rump of the former Islamic Ottoman Empire. He became its first president and was a great modernizer, but his country sits uneasily with its secular–Islamic divide.

Born Mustafa Rizi in Salonika, then a thriving port of the Ottoman Empire, the son of a customs official, he grew up to be a soldier. Nicknamed Kemal—"the perfect one"—by his mathematics teacher, he attended army cadet schools and in 1899 entered the War College in Istanbul. He graduated as a lieutenant in 1902 and was promoted captain after completing Staff College in 1905. As a young officer, he became involved in the secret Young Turk movement, which opposed the autocratic Ottoman government, and his associations with the nationalists clouded his army career.

Kemal had already seen action before World War I, in which the Ottomans sided with the Germans, but his great feat was the defense of Gallipoli in 1915, when he played a crucial role in repelling an Allied landing by British, Australian, New Zealand, and Senegalese troops. He was hailed as the "Savior of Istanbul," and the following year, after winning a battle against the Russians, he was promoted to general and given the title Pasha.

The Allied victors of World War I imposed humiliating terms on the old Ottoman Empire. Under the 1920 Treaty of Sèvres, it was broken up and occupied. Turks were not even allowed to run their own banks. The treaty gave Greece big slices of Anatolia and Thrace and set up an independent Armenian state. After the Sultan had signed it, the Supreme Allied Council in Paris invited Greece to move in "to restore order in Anatolia." However, they had not reckoned on Kemal, who had been appointed head of a small force

Hailed as the Savior of Istanbul after Gallipoli, Atatürk was promoted and given the title Pasha

Chronology

1881	Born in Salonika, March 12
1899	Enters War College in Istanbul
1905	Graduates from Staff College as captain
1911–12	Fights Italians in Libya
1915	Repulses Allied force at Gallipoli
1916	Defeats Russians on the Eastern front
1918	Overseas Ottoman withdrawal from Syria
1919	Calls on Turks to fight for independence
1920	Establishes provisional government in Ankara
1921	Defeats Greeks at Battle of Sakarya
1923	Becomes President of new Turkish state
1934	Given title Atatürk
1938	Dies in Istanbul, November 10

to suppress protest during the occupation.

Kemal, instead, had turned against the occupation, and on May 19, 1919 had called on Turks to rise up and fight for their independence. He had set up a headquarters in Ankara, the Turkish heartland, where he established a provisional government. Invasion by a foreign army to uphold an unequal treaty was just what Kemal needed. Within two years, he had driven the Greeks back into the sea, deposed the Sultan, and dealt with the Italians and French, and, with Russian assistance, crushed the Armenians and Kurds in the east. The British decided to negotiate, and Kemal secured a new deal—the 1923 Treaty of Lausanne. This time it was on equal terms, and Turkey emerged from the ashes of six centuries of Ottoman rule, a free country with Kemal as its leader. The

new Turkish Republic was proclaimed on October 29, 1923.

Kemal built the modern Turkish state. The cornerstone was secularization. Islam, long dominant in all walks of life, was confined to the mosque and the privacy of the home. The caliphate was abolished in 1924, and the law secularized. The new constitution of 1928 removed the statement that Turkey was an Islamic state. Religion was banned from public life, and the wearing of the veil was outlawed. Even the fez, a flat-topped coned cap that had originally been imported from Europe, went. The Western calendar was introduced, and Saturday

Father of Turkey

■ During the defense of Gallipoli, Kemal was hit by a piece of shrapnel, but the watch he kept in his breast pocket saved his life.
■ Kemal Atatürk is still omnipresent in Turkey, with statues of him in many places and his portrait in public buildings, and on bank notes and postage stamps.
■ More than two generations after Kemal's death, Turkey is still seeking membership of the European Union, and militants inside Turkey are determined on returning the country to Islam.

replaced the Muslim Friday as the "weekend." The Turkish Arabic script was latinized. Polygamy was outlawed and women were given the vote. Kemal's secular revolution was, in fact, so sweeping that he had transformed Turkey by the 1930s into one of the most advanced liberal states in the world.

The National Assembly conferred the title Atatürk—"Father of the Turks"—on Kemal in 1934, confirming his place in Turkish history. A lifelong heavy drinker, he died of cirrhosis of the liver in Istanbul on November 10, 1938.

Mahatma Gandhi

Mahatma Gandhi (1869–1948), nationalist leader, holy man, and great proponent of nonviolent protest, led India peacefully out of the British Empire, and shortly after died at the hands of a Hindu assassin.

Born Mohandas Karamchand Gandhi in the town of Porbandar in British-ruled India, in what is now the state of Gujarãt, Gandhi was schooled in nearby Rãjkot, where his father was prime minister to a local ruler. Married in accordance with custom at the age of thirteen, he sailed for London aged eighteen to study law, leaving behind his wife and infant son. Victorian England opened Gandhi's eyes to the realities of the industrial world, and also to philosophy and the major religions. He became a barrister in 1891 and, after trying to set up on his own in Bombay, he accepted an offer from an Indian businessman to work in South Africa.

Gandhi spent twenty-one years in South Africa, and it was there, faced with racial humiliation, that he became a political activist. A catalyst was being thrown out of a first-class railway compartment because he was a "half-

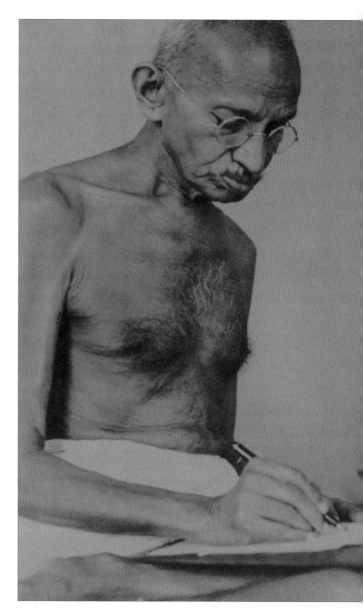

caste" Indian, even though he had a first-class ticket. Gandhi soon emerged as the leader of the South African Indian community and secured some measure of racial and political justice for his fellow Indians. In 1894 he founded the Natal Indian Congress. In South Africa, he also developed a method of nonviolent resistance, which he termed "satyagraha", and at the same time he nurtured his own distinct spiritual view of life.

An Ascetic Life

■ "Nonviolence is the greatest force at the disposal of mankind. It is mightier than the mightiest weapon of destruction devised by the ingenuity of man," Gandhi said.

■ "What do I think of Western civilization? I think it would be a very good idea."

■ Gandhi was attracted to a life of simplicity, manual labor, and austerity. He cared nothing for money, power, or sensual pleasure—only for the inner being.

■ Religion, not politics, was his primary driver. "What I have been striving and pining to achieve these thirty years," he wrote in his autobiography, "is to see God face to face."

Chronology

1869	Born at Porbandar, Gujarāt, October 2
1882	Marries a teenage bride
1888	Leaves for London to study law
1891	Becomes a barrister; sails for home
1892	Barrister in Bombay
1893	Moves to South Africa
1894	Founds Natal Indian Congress
1906	Starts Passive Resistance Movement
1915	Returns to India
1919	Amritsar Massacre; non-cooperation movement spreads nationwide
1922–4	Two years in jail
1930	Anti-salt tax Dandi March
1931	Represents National Congress in London talks
1934	Resigns leadership of National Congress
1942	Interned for two years
1947	India granted independence
1948	Assassinated in New Delhi, January 30

In 1909, on a trip back in India, Gandhi wrote a small treatise on Indian home rule. He returned to India for good in 1915 and traveled extensively, involving himself, as he had in South Africa, in numerous local struggles. He finally turned against the British after World War I and plunged into politics. Following the Amritsar Massacre in 1919, when a British army general ordered his troops to shoot several hundred unarmed demonstrators, Gandhi initiated a nationwide campaign of passive non-cooperation, including a boycott of British goods. He turned the inactive Indian National Congress into an effective movement, and assumed the mantle of India's nationalist movement. Gandhi was jailed for the first of many times in India in 1922, after delivering an impassioned indictment of British rule at his trial.

Released after two years, Gandhi set about preparing India psychologically and sociologically for independence; he spoke out against the caste system, called for inter-faith tolerance, and worked to revive a sense of national self-confidence. He preached what he called "the new science of nonviolence" based on a belief in universal love, and earned himself the title of Mahatma, or "Great Soul."

To a growing audience, he propounded his ideas on everything from hygiene and vegetarianism to education, and promoted his ideals of a utopian, socialist society.

In 1928 Gandhi called on Britain to give India dominion status. He backed up his demands in 1930 by urging Indians to refuse to pay taxes, and led a spectacular national march against the tax on salt. The British wavered and in 1931 he was sent to London for negotiations; they came to nothing and he was rearrested on his return to India. While still in prison, he started another hunger strike to protest against the government's decision to segregate India's "untouchables." On his release he vowed not to go back to his ashram until India was independent, and, after resigning the leadership of the National Congress in 1934, he set up home in Sevagram, a remote village in the very heart of the continent. He was by now a leader of unquestioned authority, and had no need of political office; politicians instead beat a path to him.

Gandhi and the Congress leadership remained neutral during World War II, but most of its members were interned in 1942 after he made a speech in which he bluntly asked the British to "quit India." With the Labour Party in power in London after the war, negotiations for independence intensified, and with them the tensions between Muslims and Hindus. Gandhi bravely walked from village to village trying to staunch the sectarian violence as up to one million people died in the run-up to independence and partition of the subcontinent in 1947, and he embarked on his final fast unto death. The fast halted rioting in Calcutta in September 1947, and persuaded both communities in Delhi to agree in January 1948 to live in "perfect amity." But a few days later Gandhi was shot dead on his way to evening prayers by Nathuram Godse, a Hindu angered at his pragmatic acceptance of the division of the subcontinent into Hindu India and Muslim Pakistan. His hands still folded in his final prayer, the dying Gandhi blessed his assassin: "Hey, Rama" (Oh, God).

"What do I think of Western civilization? I think it would be a very good idea."

Nelson Mandela

Nelson Rolihlahla Mandela (1918–) became the international symbol of the struggle to free South Africa from apartheid, and the country's first black president. A leading figure in the African National Congress civil rights group, he served twenty-seven years in jail before being freed in 1990 after President F. W. de Klerk bowed to international pressure and agreed to end apartheid.

Nelson Rolihlahla Mandela—the middle name means "troublemaker"—was the son of a Thembu tribal chief and thus to some extent shielded from the poverty inflicted on most of his fellow black South Africans by the country's racial segregationalist policy, known as apartheid. Born in the Umtata province of the Transkei, now the Eastern Cape Province, in 1918, at the age of seven he was the first of his family to attend school.

After secondary education at Healdtown School, Mandela went on to University College of Fort Hare, then South Africa's only seat of higher education for blacks, to read for a Bachelor of Arts degree. By his early twenties, though, Mandela was becoming increasingly politicized, influenced in particular by Walter Sisulu, one of the brightest young thinkers in the African National Congress (ANC). Mandela joined the organization in 1942 and, with Sisulu, Oliver Tambo, and others, played a key role in launching the ANC Youth League with the aim of broadening and radicalizing the ANC's support base. His growing radicalism cost him his place at Fort Hare, and he was obliged to complete his degree by correspondence while living in Johannesburg, working toward legal qualifications.

When the National Party won the 1948 elections on an apartheid platform, the Youth League's leadership, Mandela included, drew up

> *"I have cherished the ideal of a democratic and free society in which all persons live together in harmony"*

an action program advocating boycotts, strikes, civil disobedience, and non-cooperation in pursuit of full citizenship and direct parliamentary representation for all South Africans, regardless of race. The program was adopted as ANC policy in 1949, when Sisulu became its secretary general, Mandela joining him on the National Executive Committee the following year.

In 1952 the ANC launched a mass disobedience campaign and Mandela traveled the country organizing support, which earned him his first serious brush with the law and a six-month

Speech From the Dock

■ At his trial at Rivonia, which lasted from October 1963 to June 1964, Mandela spelled out his creed: "I have fought against white domination, and I have fought against black domination. I have cherished the ideal of a democratic and free society in which all persons live together in harmony and with equal opportunities. It is an ideal which I hope to live for and to achieve. But if needs be, it is an ideal for which I am prepared to die."

■ Mandela's wife Winnie did much to keep the ANC cause alive and transform her husband into the world's most famous political prisoner. But after his release, the couple separated and finally divorced in 1996.

■ Mandela was married again on his 80th birthday, in July 1998, to Graca Machel, widow of the first president of Mozambique.

Nelson Mandela

Chronology

1918	Born in Umtata district, Transkei, July 18
1942	Joins civil rights group the African National Congress
1943	Graduates from Fort Hare University College
1944	Helps found ANC Youth League
1952	Qualifies as lawyer, opens own law office in Johannesburg
1956	Arrested and charged with high treason, acquitted 1961
1962	Rearrested, sentenced to five years in jail
1964	Convicted of treason and sabotage, sentenced to life imprisonment
1990	Released from jail, ban on ANC lifted
1993	Awarded Nobel Peace Prize, jointly with President F. W. de Klerk
1994	Elected President in South Africa's first fully democratic general elections
1999	Retires from public life

suspended prison sentence. The same year, he opened a legal practice in Johannesburg, in partnership with Oliver Tambo.

The late 1950s saw more brushes with the law and Mandela's arrest on a charge of high treason, on which he was eventually acquitted in 1961. The Sharpeville Massacre of 1960, when sixty-seven blacks were shot dead during an anti-apartheid demonstration, had led to the banning of the ANC. In 1961, as the struggle for democratic freedoms intensified, the ANC concluded that armed struggle was its only realistic option and established Umkhonto we Sizwe (Spear of the Nation) as an armed nucleus, with Mandela as its commander. His successful evasion of the police during this period earned him the nickname the Black Pimpernel; but in 1962 his luck ran out and he was arrested and jailed for five years for illegally leaving the country to rally support. Two years later he was charged with treason and sabotage, and sentenced to life imprisonment.

Mandela was incarcerated at the notorious Robben Island prison off Cape Town, along with several other key ANC leaders. But over his eighteen years there, his international renown grew and pressure for an end to the apartheid system intensified. In 1982 he was moved to a maximum security jail near Cape Town, in much improved conditions. In 1988, after meetings with a number of international statesmen and "feelers" from the apartheid regime, Mandela entered into direct talks with the government, and in 1989 had his first meeting with President P. W. Botha. When F. W. de Klerk became president later that year, he released Walter Sisulu and other prominent ANC leaders from jail as he began dismantling the apartheid structure. Mandela met de Klerk in December, and two months later, on February 11, 1990, he was free.

The next four years saw the steady eradication of decades of repression, alongside preparations for South Africa's first fully democratic elections. Mandela and de Klerk received international recognition for the peaceful transformation when they shared the 1993 Nobel Peace Prize and in May 1994, with an overwhelming majority, Nelson Mandela became the country's first black president, governing South Africa for five years. He worked tirelessly in office and in retirement for peace and justice. Now in his nineties, Mandela is rarely seen and has been hospitalized on several occasions for ill health.

Shaka Zulu

Shaka Zulu (1787–1828) was a warrior chief who created a powerful fighting force to wipe out his enemies and establish southern Africa's Zulu Empire.

Shaka was born in 1787, the illegitimate son of Senzangakona, a chief of the then little-known Zulu tribe, and Nandi, an orphaned princess of the Langeni clan. Senzangakona repudiated Nandi, and she and Shaka went to live in exile with the Langeni, where both mother and son were treated as virtual outcasts. The Langeni drove Nandi and her son out and they found shelter with the Mtetwa. From about 1802, Shaka joined the Mtetwa army and quickly distinguished himself as a fearless and skilled fighter. He excelled in single combat, using shield and spear, and over six years rose to high rank in the Mtetwa army. On the death of Shaka's father in 1816, the Mtetwa chieftain, Dingiswayo, gave him military assistance to win back his rightful inheritance as chief of the Zulus.

Shaka had enormous ambitions for a tribe that then numbered little more than 1,500. He aimed to rule all of southern Africa and he set about building a powerful Zulu army. He established military towns and provided his army with the best training and provisions, and the strictest discipline. His soldiers were required to remain celibate, and violation of the rule was punished by death. Any soldier who showed fear in battle was instantly killed. He divided the army into regiments or impi and, like the Romans, he incorporated defeated tribes into their ranks. He also introduced women's regiments. His men could march 50 miles (80 km) in a day.

Shaka revolutionized the Zulu army's weaponry as well as its military tactics. He perfected complex battle formations to outflank and confuse his enemies, notably the "buffalo" formation, when the "horns" encircled the opposing army. It had been customary in the past for Zulu warriors to throw their spears and then withdraw; however, Shaka changed their approach to battle, and designed a stabbing spear, which forced his men to engage the enemy in close combat.

He fought bloody wars, which normally ended with the total annihilation of his enemies, uprooting thousands, and killing at least a million. He turned first on the Langeni, to avenge his childhood humiliation, impaling their leaders on the stakes of their kraals, and next he destroyed the Butelezi. After the Mtetwa chief Dingiswayo died in 1817, there was no stopping Shaka. He cleaned up the coastal areas and from 1820 set about systematically wiping out all the rival tribes on the Natal plateau—an extermination called the Mfecane or "Crushing." The Zulu Empire eventually stretched from the Cape to Tanzania.

Shaka first came into contact with Europeans in Natal in 1824, and he gave them tracts of land. He was treated for a wound by a visiting Englishman. Shaka seems to have gone totally mad following the death of his mother in 1827.

Shaka perfected complex battle formations, most notably the "buffalo" formation of "head" and "horns"

Chronology

1787	Born
1802	Shaka joins the Mtetwa army
1816	Becomes chief of the Zulu on death of his father
1817	Begins expansion of Zulu Empire
1820	Start of the Mfecane
1827	Death of his mother
1828	Murdered by his half brothers, September 22

In his grief, he slaughtered 7,000 Zulus, and no crops were planted for a year, and milk—a Zulu staple—was banned. Shaka was murdered by his half brothers in 1828. They stabbed him to death and threw his body into an empty grain pot.

The Mfecane

■ The uprooted people, victims of the Mfecane, migrated as far north as modern Tanzania and as far south as Cape Province. The devastation was so complete that the Boers passed through uninhabited empty land when they crossed Natal on their Great Trek in 1830.

■ Shaka's name, now hallowed, was originally an insult—"iShaka" was an intestinal parasite thought to be responsible for some female illnesses and said, by Zulu elders, to be the true cause of Nandi's pregnancy.

■ Zulu power endured; fifty years after his death, Shaka's army beat British regulars in the Zulu War.

Aung San Suu Kyi

Aung San Suu Kyi (1945–) is an international symbol of peaceful opposition to oppression. She has spent some fifteen years in detention or under house arrest for leading the opposition to her country's military rulers, and her tenacity and courage have earned her worldwide admiration. Awarded the Nobel Peace Prize in 1991, her most recent release from house arrest came on November 13, 2010.

Suu Kyi is the only daughter of Burma's national leader Aung San, who led his country's struggle for independence from Britain. He was assassinated in 1947 when she was just two years old. She was educated in Burma and India, where her mother was Burmese ambassador in the early 1960s. After studying politics at Delhi University, she moved to England's Oxford University for three years and graduated in 1967 with a degree in politics, philosophy, and economics (PPE). It was there that she met and later married an Oxford academic, Michael Aris. She embarked on an international career with the United Nations in New York, moving in various governmental and research roles to Bhutan, India, and Japan, before settling back in Oxford to raise her two sons. She would doubtless have remained there had her mother not fallen ill.

"Myanmar" has systematically resisted international calls to release Suu Kyi and restore democracy.

Suu Kyi returned to Myanmar (then Burma) to nurse her mother in 1988 to find her country in turmoil; a popular uprising against the military, which had seized power in 1962, was being ruthlessly suppressed. Thousands died, and Suu Kyi rose to the challenge. "I could not, as my father's daughter, remain indifferent to what was going on," she said at her first mass rally of half a million people in front of Yangon's famous Shwedagon Pagoda. "This national crisis could in fact be called the second struggle for independence."

She founded an opposition party, the National League for Democracy, in 1988, and was arrested in 1989 for allegedly inciting violence. The following year, 1990, her National League for Democracy won a landslide victory in elections, capturing 82 percent of the vote. But the military, calling itself the State Law and Order Restoration Council, refused to hand over power. The Burmese generals placed her in solitary confinement, and she was barred from seeing any visitors, including her family.

Medal of Freedom

■ Suu Kyi models her struggle for the restoration of democracy on the ways of Mahatma Gandhi, and above all on his commitment to nonviolence as a means of achieving one's political ends. She always wears a flower in her hair in public.

■ In 2000, U.S. President Bill Clinton conferred the Presidential Medal of Freedom, America's highest civilian honor, on Suu Kyi for her commitment to democracy.

■ Under house arrest, Suu Kyi kept herself busy by studying and exercising. She meditated, practiced her French and Japanese, and played the piano.

■ In March 2012 she campaigned for reform of the 2008 Constitution, for greater protection of democratic rights, and for the establishment of an independent judiciary.

114

When she was awarded the Nobel Peace Prize in 1991, her sons picked it up on her behalf. The judges called her "one of the most extraordinary examples of civil courage in Asia."

She was released in 1995, but kept under strict surveillance, and then rearrested and confined to her house again in September 2000. Her husband had died from cancer in 1999, having not seen her for three years. She was offered the chance to travel to England for his funeral, but she refused, knowing the military would not allow her back into Myanmar. He had been refused a visa to visit her.

Upon her release in May 2002, she resumed campaigning for the National League for Democracy, only to be placed under house arrest once again at her home in Yangon in September 2003, after undergoing major surgery. She was released in 2010 and in January 2012 registered to contest a seat in the special parliamentary elections to be held in April 2012.

Chronology

1945	Born in Rangoon (now Yangon), June 19
1947	General Aung San assassinated
1948	Burma gains independence
1962	General Ne Win seizes power
1967	Graduates from Oxford University
1988	Returns to Burma
1988	Forms National League for Democracy
1989	Placed under house arrest
1990	National League wins 82 percent of vote
1991	Wins Nobel Peace Prize
1995	Freed from house arrest
1999	Her husband Michael Aris dies
2010	Released from house arrest
2012	Contested seat in parliamentary elections

Spartacus

Spartacus (c.120–71 BCE) was a Roman slave and gladiator, born in Thrace, who led a major rebellion against Rome.

A Thracian by birth, Spartacus served in the Roman army but somehow ran foul of authority—possibly he deserted—and he and his wife were sold into slavery. They were taken to the slave-market in Rome and were both bought by Lentulus Batiates, who ran a school for gladiators in Capua. Gladiators were trained to fight in the arena, many of them to the death, in order to entertain the Romans.

Once in Capua, Spartacus determined to break out. "If we must fight, we might as well fight for our freedom," he was reported to have said. Using spits and chopping knives seized from the kitchens, seventy-eight gladiators fought their way out on the streets and into open country, where they defeated a small force sent to capture them. They now had weapons and they established a camp on top of Mount Vesuvius, inside the crater of the dormant volcano.

An army of 3,000 men now marched from Rome and surrounded him. But the gladiators, using ropes that they had twisted from vines to lower themselves down an impregnable cliff face, took them by surprise and captured the entire Roman force. The Senate in Rome hurriedly dispatched two more forces to subdue the slaves, but both were routed. A legend was born, and more and more slaves flocked to join Spartacus; by 72 BCE, less than a year after the escape from Capua, Spartacus was commanding an army of 70,000 men. Most of Rome's armies were fighting abroad, so the regular troops in Italy were outnumbered by the rebels.

An army of 3,000 marched from Rome; Spartacus took them by surprise and captured them all

Spartacus could now roam the length and breadth of Italy and he set his heart on breaking out over the Alps to freedom. But he couldn't persuade the Gauls and Germans who had joined his forces to follow him. Meanwhile, Rome elected a new general to lead a force against Spartacus—Marcus Licinius Crassus. A rich man, he seems to have been one of the few high-ranking men in Rome willing to risk his reputation against a bunch of slaves.

Crassus raised an army of six legions. He sent his lieutenant Mummius on ahead with two legions to harass the slaves and with strict orders not to fight a pitched battle. But Mummius disobeyed and was routed. Crassus sentenced the defeated legions to be decimated—lots were

Revolutionary Hero

■ Spartacus is often hailed as a champion of the masses and a social revolutionary. In fact there is no evidence that he wanted anything except his freedom and to return home. Nonetheless, his name was frequently invoked by revolutionaries—most notably the German Communist Spartakus League, led by Rosa Luxemburg and Karl Liebknecht, who were both killed in an abortive uprising against the German government in 1919.

■ Just as the original gladiators stirred the crowd's imagination in the Roman amphitheaters, so do rather gentler representations of their prowess today. Spartacus' rebellion against Rome inspired a 1960 Hollywood blockbuster, named simply *Spartacus*, directed by Stanley Kubrick and starring Kirk Douglas as Spartacus, and a 1968 Russian ballet, with music composed by Aram Khachaturian.

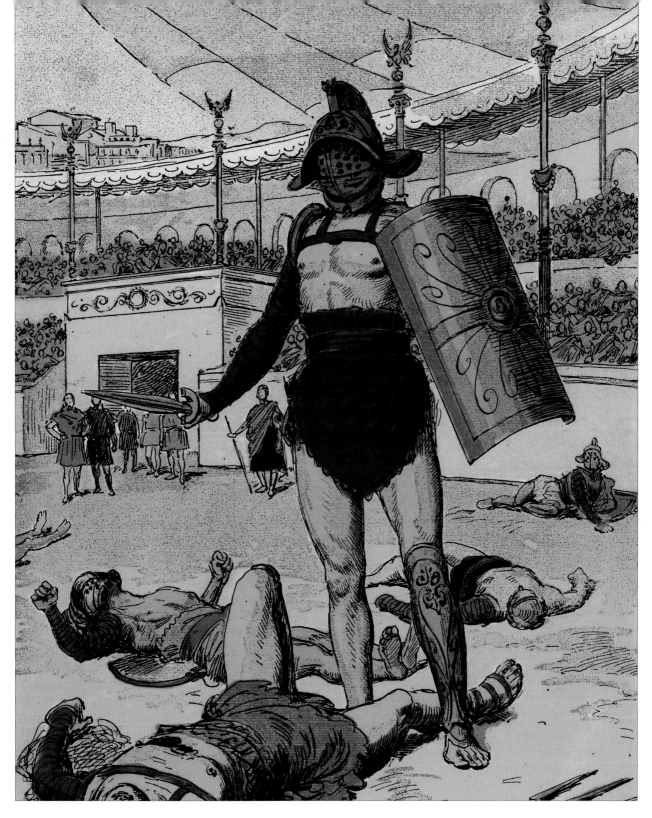

drawn for one in every ten surviving soldiers to be put to the sword.

Spartacus moved south, where he made an unsuccessful bid to escape to Sicily. Crassus closed in on him, and was joined by Pompey's army which had just returned to Italy from Spain. Early in 71 BCE, Spartacus decided to risk fighting a decisive battle against the Romans. He knew it would be winner-take-all and famously killed his own horse before the fighting started, saying that if he won the day he would get a better horse and if he lost he would have no need of a mount. At Petelia in Lucania, the Romans prevailed and Spartacus was first wounded and then killed. All the rebel slaves perished, except for 6,000 who were captured and crucified along the road from Capua to Rome.

Chronology

120 BCE	Estimated date of Spartacus's birth
73 BCE	Spartacus leads rebellion of gladiators
72 BCE	Gladiators defeat Roman forces
71 BCE	Spartacus defeated and killed

Giuseppe Garibaldi

Giuseppe Garibaldi (1807–82), a nationalist leader and guerrilla fighter who helped create the modern state of Italy, was a swashbuckling adventurer whose exploits made him a hero on two continents, Europe and South America.

Garibaldi was the self-educated son of a fisherman from Nice, who started life as a humble merchant seaman. His defining achievement was to lead a guerrilla army to free Italy from foreign occupation; in addition he packed in fourteen years fighting battles in South America, was offered a Union command by U.S. President Abraham Lincoln in the American Civil War, and took part in the 1870–71 Franco-Prussian war.

Garibaldi's legendary crusade to liberate southern Italy started in May 1860 when he commandeered two old paddle steamers in Genoa and led a volunteer force of 1,070 guerrilla "Redshirts," so-called because of their uniform, to victory against 12,000 regular soldiers in Sicily.

Three months later he crossed the Straits of Messina to the Italian mainland, routing the armies of the Bourbon monarch on the banks of the Volturno River on October 26 1860 to capture Naples and win the whole of the south for the new kingdom of Italy.

Italy as a nation did not exist when Garibaldi was born. It was divided into warring states, dukedoms, principalities, and territories ruled by the popes in Rome, and it was also dominated by its two powerful neighbors—France and Austria.

Inspired by the early Italian nationalists, Garibaldi, by now a merchant sea captain and serving in the Piedmontese navy, embarked on his long revolutionary career by taking part in a mutiny that was intended to provoke an uprising against the Austrians in 1834.

The uprising failed: Garibaldi was sentenced to death *in absentia* and escaped to South America, where he lived from 1836 to 1848, taking part in a number of uprisings in Brazil and fighting for Uruguay in its war of independence with Argentina.

Garibaldi raced back to Europe at the outbreak of the 1848 revolutions to fight for the Risorgimento, or resurrection of Italy, and together with Giuseppe Mazzini he established a republic in Rome before it was crushed by French troops in 1849. His Brazilian wife, Anita, who had fought alongside him, died during the campaign, in which Garibaldi refused to accept defeat and displayed exemplary courage and outstanding leadership. He got away, first to Tangier, then to the United States, where he became an American citizen, and finally to Peru where, for a time, he plied his original trade as a ship's captain.

Garibaldi came back to Europe in 1854, and four years later joined yet another attempt to reunify Italy. This one succeeded—thanks largely to Garibaldi's extraordinary military leadership. In South America, he had become a master of guerrilla warfare, capable of beating professional forces by hit-and-run and ambush.

Garibaldi became a master of guerrilla warfare, beating professional forces by hit-and-run and ambush

Chronology

1807	Born in Nice on July 4
1834	Sentenced to death for Piedmont uprising
1834–48	South America
1848–9	Revolution and failure of Rome republic
1859	Defeats Austrians in Alps
1860	Conquest of Sicily and Naples
1871	Wins Battle of Dijon with French
1874	Elected to Italian Parliament
1882	Dies on island of Caprera on June 2

Giuseppe Garibaldi

Garibaldi went to war one more time, fighting alongside the French against the Prussians in 1871, and earning himself a seat in France's National Assembly.

He was also elected to Italy's Parliament in 1874. He lived out his old age on Caprera as a highly respected statesman on both sides of the Atlantic and a grand old man of national revolution—the "hero of two worlds."

He defeated the Austrians in the Alps in 1859, and set out for the south with his famous "Thousand." After the fall of Naples, and impatient to complete the reunification of Italy, Garibaldi launched two further abortive military expeditions, to seize Venice and Rome, being wounded and captured in the process. International politics eventually forced the Austrians to cede Venice and the French to withdraw from Rome, and Italy became a unified and free country again in 1870.

The Redshirts

■ Garibaldi's fighters were famous for their red shirts. It was in Uruguay that he first dressed his men in red shirts, obtained from a factory in Montevideo which had intended to export them to the slaughter houses of Argentina.

■ Garibaldi's memoirs, *Autobiography of Giuseppe Garibaldi*, were published in 1887 and had a far-reaching impact, inspiring, among others, the movement for independence in India.

■ In addition to being hailed as a hero and the "sword" of Italian reunification in his own country, Garibaldi is honored with a statue in New York City. He brought London to a standstill when he made a triumphal visit to Britain in 1864.

Vladimir Lenin

Vladimir Lenin (1870–1924) was one of the world's greatest revolutionary leaders and the founder of the first Marxist State, the Soviet Union. He became a universal symbol of a communist ideology that spawned revolutionary movements around the world.

Vladimir Ilyich Ulyanov was born into a privileged class in nineteenth-century Russia. His father, Ilya, an Inspector for Elementary Schools, was married to Maria Alexandrovna, daughter of a wealthy Jewish physician. Lenin was one of six children; he was hard-working at school and enjoyed outdoor sports. His youth was shattered in 1887 when his older brother Alexander was arrested and hanged for plotting to assassinate Tsar Alexander—an event that set Lenin on the road to revolution.

Lenin enrolled at Kazan University in the same year but he was quickly expelled for illegal opposition activities, and exiled to his grandfather's estate in the village of Kokushkino. In exile, he started reading European revolutionary writers, notably Karl Marx, and became a self-professed Marxist. After qualifying as a lawyer, he moved in 1893 to St Petersburg, where he plunged into underground opposition to the Tsarist regime.

Lenin helped set up a Marxist workers' organization in St Petersburg, for which he was jailed for fifteen months, along with his wife-to-be Nadezhda Krupskaya, before being sent into exile for three years to Siberia. Released in 1900, he fled abroad where he joined fellow revolutionaries in starting a newspaper, *Iskra* (The Spark), and in 1902 published his seminal work *What Is To Be Done?*

Lenin had by now come round to believing that revolution would only succeed if it were led by a small professional group—in effect controlled from the top. His insistence on professional revolutionary cadres split the main opposition grouping, the Russian Social Democratic Labor Party. Two powerful factions emerged at the party's 1903 Congress, which was held in London—the Mensheviks (Russian for minority), who opposed Lenin, and the Bolsheviks (Russian for majority), who supported him by a small majority.

Lenin was abroad when revolution erupted in 1905; he returned home after it had lost momentum and in its repressive aftermath he again went into exile. The Mensheviks and Bolsheviks bickered for years over the failure of the 1905 revolution and split irrevocably in 1912. Lenin, meanwhile, faced hardship in exile. He continued writing, producing his major philosophical work *Materialism and Empirio-Criticism* in 1909. When World War I broke out, he called on workers to unite against it to "transform the imperialist war into a civil war." Their duty was to destroy capitalism, not fight each other.

Rolls-Royce Revolutionary

■ Lenin had a passion for Rolls-Royces. He owned nine, including the world's only half-track Rolls-Royce, adapted with skis at the front for driving in the snow.

■ "Bread not war" was one of Lenin's most famous slogans.

■ "I'll make them pay for this! I swear it!" Lenin is supposed to have said on learning of his brother's execution.

■ After his death, Lenin's body was embalmed and laid in a crystal coffin in a mausoleum by the Kremlin, where it still lies in state—almost the last symbolic remnant of the Soviet Union. Visitors still wait in line to see his body today.

disgruntled peasantry, who had borne the brunt of the war, and a decree of nationalization of industry. Lenin's overriding concern, however, was to stay in power, and the infant Soviet state had first to contend with a brutal civil war, which lasted from 1918 to 1921, as well as devastating famine, which killed millions.

After the war, Lenin had to compromise to ensure the survival of communism, and issued a New Economic Policy, which aimed to restore a degree of market economy. But he suffered the first of three strokes in May 1922 and thereafter lost direct control of government.

"Peace, bread, land, and all power to the soviets"

A master strategist, he did not live long enough to see his dream turn into a nightmare under his successor, Joseph Stalin.

Lenin missed the outbreak of the February 1917 revolution, which overthrew the Tsarist regime; he sneaked back into Russia through Germany one month later in a sealed train. Russia was in the hands of a weak provisional bourgeois government, led by Alexander Kerensky, and her army was still floundering in the war. Lenin seized the moment, and called for outright revolution; and the Bolshevik party emerged from an emergency congress with the slogan: "All Power to the Soviets."

A workers' uprising in July failed and Lenin spent August and September in Finland, pressing his case for armed insurrection in the capital. It finally broke out on October 25—"The October Revolution"—and a few days later Lenin was elected Chairman of the People's Commissars, de facto head of government.

Lenin gradually, but cautiously, consolidated the power of the new Soviet state. He ended the war with Germany, accepting punitive terms, and started to implement what had up until then just been a dream on paper—the communist state. It began with mass transfers of land to the

Chronology

1870	Born in Simbirsk, on the River Volga, April 22
1887	Lenin's brother Alexander executed in May
1895	Arrested in St Petersburg
1897	First exile
1898	Marries Nadezhda Krupskaya
1899	Second exile in Siberia
1900	Release of Lenin and publication of *Iskra*
1902	Publication of *What Is To Be Done?*
1905	Outbreak of First Russian Revolution
1917	February, Russian Revolution overthrows Tsar; October, Bolsheviks instigate second Revolution
1918	Bolsheviks become Communist Party; outbreak of civil war and execution of royal family
1921	New Economic Policy
1924	Lenin dies in Gorky, January 21

Lech Walesa

Lech Walesa (1943–) led the Polish workers' revolt in the shipyards in Gdansk that gave birth to the Solidarity free trade union and eventually brought down Communist rule in Poland. A Nobel Peace Prize laureate, he became president of his country.

The son of a carpenter, Walesa became an electrician at the huge Lenin shipyards in Gdansk, northern Poland, in 1967. The 1970 food riots, in which a number of demonstrators were killed outside the shipyard gates, led him to join the underground trade union movement, in effect the illegal opposition to the Communists. He lost his job after taking part in a new wave of worker protests in 1976, and spent the next four years working mainly as an underground activist, and playing cat and mouse with the Polish police.

His moment came in the summer of 1980 when Polish workers, displaying a new confidence in their opposition to the deeply unpopular Soviet-backed Communists following the election of Polish Pope John Paul II, staged strikes across the country. Walesa clambered over the fence and took control of the sit-in protest at the Lenin shipyard, and he was soon leading an inter-factory strike committee, which threw down the gauntlet to the beleaguered Communist government in Warsaw. The committee, naming itself Solidarity, demanded the right to form a free trade union and the right to strike—freedoms unheard of in the East Bloc, where the ruling Communist Party was meant to control everything.

Walesa, with his hallmark walrus moustache, became a global hero overnight. He was brash, tough, and charming, and ably supported by other more intellectual activists; during tough negotiations, and backed by a national strike,

A symbol of protest, ultimately Walesa was too much the impatient revolutionary to play the statesman

Chronology

1943	Born in Popowo, near Wroclawek, September 29
1980	Leads workers' strikes, founds Solidarity
1981	Polish Communists impose martial law
1983	Awarded Nobel Peace Prize
1990	Elected President of Poland
1995	Loses presidential election; returns to shipyard
2000	Again loses presidential election; quits politics

they wore down the Communists. The Solidarity Free Trade Union was born on August 31, 1980 and under Walesa's leadership over the next sixteen months its membership grew to some ten million. Solidarity had become a mass protest against Communist rule, threatening the very foundations of Soviet control over eastern Europe.

Pressured by Moscow, the Communists struck back on December 13, 1981, imposed martial law, and suspended Solidarity. Walesa and his top aides were arrested, and he spent eleven months in detention. Solidarity went underground with Walesa still in charge, and the protests continued. Walesa was awarded the Nobel Peace Prize in 1983 but, fearing that he would be unable to return, he sent his wife Danuta to Oslo to receive it. A new wave of unrest in 1988, and the glasnost liberalization in Moscow, forced the Communists back to negotiating with Walesa. Solidarity was re-legalized and won all the free seats in partial parliamentary elections in 1989. The following year, in December 1990, Walesa was elected President of Poland in a landslide victory.

Walesa was less successful in the largely ceremonial role of President. He was frustrated by his lack of power and indulged in some erratic behavior, and his plain speech and confrontational style, combined with opposition to the new abortion law, lost him reelection in 1995. He briefly returned to the shipyard—more as a gesture of protest—and ran again for President in 2000. This time he gained less than 1 percent of the vote, and he announced afterward that he was quitting politics.

Walesa was both a great symbol of protest and a great leader of protest, but in the end he was too much the impatient revolutionary, and neither subtle nor shrewd enough to be a great statesman.

Following the Pope

■ Lech Walesa always paid tribute to the role of Pope John Paul II in Poland's march to freedom. The pope's visit in 1979 had shown ordinary Poles that there were still millions of believers who rejected the officially atheist Communists, and this gave them the confidence to launch the nationwide strikes the following summer.

■ When Walesa signed the free trade union agreement with the Communists, he used a pen with a big picture of the pope.

■ The Polish workers' underground movement KOR also played a major part in fomenting and organizing the 1980 strikes.

Glossary

anti-Semitism Feelings of fear or hatred toward Jews, and the expression of those feelings as prejudice and discrimination.

apartheid A political system (literally meaning "aparthood") that enforced the separation of people of different races, and discrimination against those of non-white backgrounds. This system was in place in South Africa between 1948 and 1994.

asceticism The exercise of rigorous self-discipline and self-denial, often in a religious context. Ascetics avoid practices and possessions associated with pleasure, such as food and others' company. They often adopt this lifestyle as a way of achieving spiritual wisdom or rewards.

autodidact Someone who has taught themselves, rather than taking instruction from a teacher.

Blitz (the) A period of intense German aerial bombing of Great Britain and Northern Ireland during World War II. This is an abbreviation of the German term *blitzkrieg*, meaning "lightning war."

Brahmin A member of the highest caste—the priest caste—in traditional Hinduism.

Buddhism A religion founded in Northern India in the 5th century BCE by Siddartha Gautama. According to Buddhism, all living things are trapped in a perpetual and painful cycle of death and rebirth. The ultimate goal of life is to transcend our worldly existence, by achieving a state of ultimate enlightenment called Nirvana.

civil rights movement A movement for the equality before the law of people of all racial backgrounds. This movement was at its most prominent between the 1950s and 1980s.

communism A political theory originating with Karl Marx, according to which property and resources should be communally owned, and wealth should be distributed according to people's needs. In practice, communist states have been characterized by government ownership of resources, rather than communal ownership.

coup d'état The sudden and illegal overthrow of a government by force. The original, French meaning of the phrase is "blow to the state."

demagogue A political leader who exploits the prejudices and emotions of his or her audience rather than making factually accurate arguments.

fascism A political movement characterized by authoritarianism and a belief in the supremacy of one national or racial group above others. The term "fascism" was originally applied to Mussolini's Italy (1922–43), but has since been used more broadly.

federalist Related to a political union between states, whereby some policies (such as foreign policy) are controlled by a central governing body, and others are determined by individual states.

glasnost A movement toward increased transparency and consultation in government, introduced in the USSR by Mikhail Gorbachev. *Glasnost* in Russian means "openness."

guerrilla warfare A form of warfare in which a small group of combatants, including armed civilians, takes on a larger, conventional army. This kind of combat is characterized by the use of ambushes, sabotage, and tactics favoring speed and surprise.

infidel A derogatory term for someone who has non-mainstream religious beliefs, or no religious beliefs.

Inquisition, the A system of religious courts created by Pope Gregory IX (circa 1232) to discover and persecute those holding heretical (which is to say, non-mainstream Christian) beliefs. The Inquisition was most active in France and Italy and was notorious for its use of torture.

junta A government controlled by military leaders who have taken power by force.

monotheism Belief in the existence of just one God.

nationalization The practice of transferring the control of assets such as industries or property from private to government control.

perestroika The political movement, championed in the USSR by Mikhail Gorbachev, of restructuring the system of government to move away from central planning and take greater account of economic markets.

proscription The practice of forbidding.

Risorgimento The political movement for the unification of Italy, which was finally achieved in 1870.

secularization The change from a society with strong links to religious organizations to a society without such links.

socialism A political movement that advocates the shared ownership of industries and resources by the community.

suffrage The right to vote in elections.

vassal Under the medieval feudal system, someone who has been granted a plot of land in exchange for service to a lord.

workhouse An institution where poverty-stricken people were given lodgings in return for their labor.

Zionism A political movement which originally advocated the existence of a Jewish state of Israel, and which now advocates the protection of that state.

For Further Reading

Johnson, Paul. *Churchill*. New York, NY: Penguin, 2010.

Mandela, Nelson. *Conversations with Myself*. New York, NY: Farrar, Straus and Giroux, 2010.

Stracchey, Lytton. *Queen Victoria: A Life*. New York, NY: Tauris Parke, 2012.

Whitney, David C. *American Presidents: Biographies of the Chief Executives from George Washington to Barack Obama*. New York, NY: Readers Digest, 2012.

Web Sites

Due to the changing nature of Internet links, Rosen Publishing has developed an online list of Web sites related to the subject of this book. This site is updated regularly. Please use this link to access the list:

http://www.rosenlinks.com/gph/leader

Index

The page references to people in bold, as Alexander the Great **60–61,** refer to the main entries for those individuals

Acknowledgments

Picture Credits
All images © Hulton Getty Images Ltd except:
pp. 6, 24, 26, 34, 98 © Topham Picturepoint;
pp. 58, 114 © Topham/AP;
pp. 110, 116 © TopFoto;
pp. 12, 112 © The British Library/HIP;
p. 22 ©Topham/Fotomas;
p. 88 © Topham/Imageworks.

Contributing Editors
Michael Fowke, Peter Jenkins, Neil Edward John, Emma Maurice, Marina Mooney, Felix Pryor, Dim Robbins, Richard Shaw, Barry Simpson, Benita Stoney, Richard Tames, Gail Turner, John Whelan, Paul Whittle.